# Bounce Back

Finding Joy During Times of Adversity

by

Jack Wilson Ryser

Bounce Back: Finding Joy During Times of Adversity

My greatest joy has come from my
sweet daughters, Alexandria, Jacqueline,
and Jamie. Thank you, my angels for your
support and love.

# Contents

# Introduction

When I was six years old, some friends and I decided to sneak away to a park a few miles from our home. Now when you are six, a few miles seems like the other side of the planet. We were going to a park where there was this fantastic hill usually popular in the winter for sledding, but this spring day we were going to ride our bikes down it. At that time my mom was a single parent and was at work, and she would have never let me go. I was certain I could be home before she got home, and she would never know I was gone.

I had never gone more than a few blocks away from my home, so I just followed my friends as we traversed our way through the residential streets to the beautiful park. When we finally got there, we were all excited to get riding on the hill. None of us were brave enough to go to the top of the hill, so we just kept riding down the side, which was certainly fast enough and fun enough for everyone...but me. I decided it was time to take on the top of the hill. I pushed my bike up to the top, straddled it, and peered over the edge. To this day, I remember looking down that steep hill. The first several feet were almost straight down. I was scared to death, but there could be no turning back now. I had my group of friends staring at me, and peer pressure was now in full swing.

Finally, I harnessed my fear and pushed off. Immediately it felt like I was traveling a hundred miles an hour. Now at this point of the story, I know all of you are going to think that I made it to the bottom of the hill, and this was a lesson in facing one's fears head on. Nope, that isn't this story. About half way down the hill at top speed I lost control of my bike and crashed. Frankly I don't remember the next several seconds as I was knocked out. But moments later I was at the bottom of the hill twisted up with my bike, having tumbled relentlessly the remaining distance down the hill. As I came to, I could see through my slightly opened, dazed eyes the feet of the half-dozen friends circled around me. One of them yelled, "He's dead!" and they all ran off and left me alone.

There I was, six years old, a few miles from home, suffering with a concussion, my bike barely able to ride, and uncertain how to get home. But I knew I had to try, so I got on the Sting-Ray bike, with the ever-so-popular sissy bar on the back, with handle bars now bent, and I started the trip back. After a few wrong turns, I ultimately meandered my way home. I don't think my mom ever knew how I got hurt.

Life is very much like this story. We may sit at the top of a hill, stricken with fear, and push off, only to find our fear realized as we crash and burn. People may scoff at us, yell at us, or even desert us. But we rise up, heal our wounds, and look for the next hill, having become a little wiser and more prepared, and hopefully, knowing how to find joy and happiness regardless of the "hills" in our life.

I help people find wealth and abundance that

they have never experienced. I help them enjoy deeper and more meaningful relationships, and I help them find emotional and spiritual health. How do I do all those things? In reality I don't. I simply help people understand how to allow themselves to be happy, and in so doing, people enjoy success in their careers, relationships, and personal lives. Happiness brings success in a person's life, not the other way around. Success does not bring happiness; happiness brings success. Notice I also said, "I help people *allow* themselves to be happy." People don't find happiness, it isn't lost; it is right there waiting for them to let it in. Unfortunately, many of us unknowingly have built up walls maintaining our own unhappiness.

We have all said what I call "If onlys." You know, things like "if only I had (fill in the blank), I would be happy." A better job, relationship, home, car, more money, etc. The list goes on forever. The thing about "If onlys" is that they never do solve the problem of happiness. Once you get that better job, you want an even better job. Once you get that nicer home, you will want an even better one. Unfortunately, nothing outside of you can make unhappiness go away permanently. You may find momentary relief from things, but true happiness must come from within. There is nothing earth shattering or revolutionary about that statement; we have all heard this before. Happiness comes from within. If you are like me, you can accept that fact easily, however, for years finding happiness inside of me felt nearly impossible.

In this book I share with you my journey to be happy. I needed to know how to develop happiness from within. Waiting for life to get easy before I could be happy was not working out. It never got easy! I found that by identifying specific thoughts and actions that I could implement in my life, happiness inevitably followed, regardless of the adversity in my life. Today, even though there is certainly adversity in my life, I have a joy and inner peace I didn't know existed. I am happy.

First, let me tell you how I got here.

Chapter 1

# How I Got Here

It was November 26, 1996, two days before
Thanksgiving. I came home early from work to see if I
could help Kameo. We had spoken on the phone a
couple hours earlier and she mentioned that she was
feeling a little better, though it would quickly become
apparent that was just her wishful thinking. I came
home and saw all the symptoms I had seen many times
before: very high fever, joint pain, and weakness. This
was a serious lupus flare. I knew the plan of action. It
was one we had taken many times before during our
ten-year marriage. We would go to the hospital, get
fluids into her, break her fever, spend a few days
recovering, and then come home. She would really hate
spending Thanksgiving in the hospital, I thought.

I asked Kameo's mother to take her to the
hospital while I dropped our girls off at my parents'
home. As I helped her into her mother's car, she

whispered into my ear, "Thanksgiving is my favorite holiday." Little did I know those would be the last words my wife would speak to me, and Thanksgiving would never be the same.

The doctor asked to sit with me privately for a moment. "We have tried but it is now time to make a decision. We can continue to keep her alive, but it is only a matter of time before she passes."

"How can this be happening?" I asked myself. "Her health has been the best it has been in years. She is only thirty-five; we have three young daughters!" There were all kinds of reasons why *she* shouldn't die.

None of those reasons mattered.

I hugged her, whispered through my tears the love I felt for her...and said good-bye. The breathing tube was removed and she slowly slipped away.

The confusion of this moment will forever haunt me. What do I do now? I mean, right now! Do I stay with the body of my loving wife, or do I hurry home to see my children? You never think of such things. It was 11:20 p.m., I had spent many late nights at the hospital, helping my wife recover from lupus flares. This night was different. She wasn't coming home. How do I tell the children? They won't understand; they are only eight, six, and two years old. Mom is their world. What about a funeral, am I supposed to plan that? I don't have a burial plot, a tombstone...now what? I had so many questions, most of which were simply my way of not feeling the unbearable pain of losing my sweet wife.

I only remember walking down a long hall of the

hospital. It had off-white, cream-colored walls with little regard to décor or style. It was unmemorable and sterile. As I drove home, I wondered how to tell the girls that Mom wasn't coming home. Eight-year-old Allie will understand death. She had been born in a whirlwind of sick days and hospital stays. She knew Mom's body never quite worked right. We had spoken of heaven and the love of a Heavenly Father her entire life, but we never had done this. We had never talked about her mother not coming home. Jackie at six years old would struggle to make sense of all of this. While she had sung songs of heaven and God in church classes, the ambiguity of it all would certainly not help her find comfort. Jamie at two years old would only know that the person she relied on for nearly everything in her world would not be there anymore. She wouldn't know why; she just would know she was gone.

I drove into my parents' driveway. They had always quickly stepped in to take the girls when we rushed to the hospital. I knew there was peace in their home at that moment because they were unaware of Kameo's death. Peace that would be shattered very soon. I walked into their home and was greeted with the concerned faces of my parents. "She is gone," I blurted out harshly. Tears and stunned silence enveloped the room.

It was only a few minutes until eight-year-old Allie stumbled into to the room, wiping the sleep from her eyes, having just awakened. "Hi, Daddy," she said. "Hi, Angel," I said, my heart filled with pain. "Come here." She climbed up on my lap and wrapped her soft, delicate arms around me. We hugged for a moment. "Angel, Mommy was really sick and her body just couldn't get better." Following that moment were the tears and sorrow of a newly widowed husband and a motherless child.

As a single father I poured myself into my children's lives. They were all that mattered to me. As the youngest child in a family of four boys, I really didn't know much about girls. It was time to learn. I quit my job at a local radio station selling advertising so I could be home with the girls. My wife had been able to be a stay-at-home mother, and I wanted to be there for them during the difficult days that lay ahead. I decided to start a small media buying firm and work from the spare bedroom in my house.

Did you know there is a book out there called *Braids and Bows*? It became my new best friend. Every morning I would slowly and methodically pull out *The Book,* as it became known, and step-by-step do the girl's hair according to the directions and pictures outlined. I was a French-curling genius by the time Allie, my oldest, started to take over the hair duties.

Allie was starting to mature. It was time for her first bra. I could handle this. It was not like I hadn't seen a bra before. So off I went to the local Target on my quest to find the perfect ten-year-old's bra. I slowly meandered into the girls' underwear department. On a freestanding wall hung display after display of adolescent undergarments. As I stood there peering at the bras in clearly a state of confusion, I became very aware of my maleness. There were three mothers, approximately the same age as I was, shopping for their little budding flowers. Their gazes went from the wall of underwear to glimpses of me. More and more they were staring at me instead of looking at the wall of underwear. Their piercing looks started to make me feel as if I was some predatory pervert on a sick prowl. I had wandered into a forbidden area in a department store that male adults simply aren't allowed, the children's underwear department. I had a choice at that moment. I could ask a question. "Excuse me, Miss, what should I be looking for in a first bra?" Or perhaps I could say something intelligent. "My goodness, this one looks like it will be very comfortable *and* supportive."

There was a third option. Grab an entire rack of bras, throw them in the cart, buy them all, and get the heck out of there. I opted for that option. Essentially, I spent two hundred bucks on my daughter's first bra.

I loved my experiences as a father. Even the awkward, difficult tasks helped me develop a closeness to my girls that perhaps under different circumstances I would not have enjoyed. However, an unfortunate thing happened during those next years. Being both a great father *and* mother never allowed me to focus on myself. I never found time for feeling the sadness of the events. I never found time to feel the passion for my own life. The trap for me was that there seemed to be an unspoken heroism in completely sacrificing oneself for his children. Everywhere I went I had children in tow. It seemed that someone would praise me for my efforts wherever I turned. It felt like a noble effort. Single mothers do it all the time and often don't get the recognition that I did. That simply deepened my commitment to the role as a parent, and fostered an increased neglect of myself and personal ambitions. Simply, nothing else mattered. Now, as I write this some fifteen years later, I realize that it wasn't necessary to forget myself. The sweet relationship I have with my daughters, now all adults, would have been nurtured because of my love for them. Not because I forgot my own pain, passions, and ambitions.

I also am aware that I am not alone in these mistakes; many people make this error. Regardless of the road we have traveled in our life—divorce, death, addiction, etc.—we often suppress ourselves. We suppress pain, we are unwilling to accept risk, and fear can dominate our existence. All the while, each day passes and we are no closer to living a fulfilling life today than we were yesterday. Day after day it continues until we realize we are on a road to nowhere.

When I was only four years old, my family, including aunts, uncles, and cousins, went on a vacation to Mesa Verde National Park. We found a short trail that took us to a picnic area surrounded by the beautiful trees of the forest. It was a perfect place. It was isolated, and no other people were around. After enjoying each other's company for an hour, it was time to clean up, walk down to the car, and get to the next adventure. My cousin Bruce was several years older than I was. As everyone was packing he decided to run to the restroom adjacent to the picnic area. I followed him as young boys do with older boys. I quietly sat outside the restroom waiting for him to come back out. I waited...and waited. Everyone had started down the trail, and there I sat alone. Somehow Bruce had left the restroom without me seeing him, and I had been left behind.

I started down the trail to find my family and it quickly ended. I had taken the wrong path. I retraced my steps back to the picnic area and still there was no one there, and now I couldn't find the trail I needed to follow to find my family. At the age of four, one is not well trained in the appropriate response to being lost. Rather than just sit there and wait until someone finally realized I was gone, I panicked and started running into the forest, trying to find the trail. I ran and I ran for what eventually became hours. I was lost in a national park and was nowhere near where I originally was lost.

So now it became the story of the day. A little boy was lost in the forest and the search was on, complete with forest rangers, volunteers, and distraught family members. One thing to note is how my family must have felt. Just three years earlier my cousin was on a camping trip with his Boy Scout troop in Zion National Park in southern Utah and was killed in a flash flood. They never found his body. Now I was lost in a national park. I can only imagine the fear that my family must have endured.

To this day, I can still see the trees in my mind

and feel my heart race with fear as if it happened just yesterday. After running for what seemed like hours, I stumbled onto a paved road. At least I had the good sense to start walking on that road rather than continue in the trees. I was crying and had been crying for some time, when I heard a car coming. I remember specifically thinking, "Should I keep crying and hopefully the car will stop? But I'm a big boy, and big boys don't cry." It was 1966 and apparently boys of that era got the foolish message at a very young age that they weren't supposed to cry. I got over that in a hurry and I decided to cry and cry hard! The car stopped.

I was rescued.

There are times in our life when we feel lost and forgotten. It happens to us all. The key will depend on how we respond to the *forest* of life. We can feel sorry for ourselves and stay in the trees, or we can take steps to help ourselves and get rescued.

It took me many years to recognize I was in the trees and what it takes to be rescued, what it takes to live a life filled with passion and fulfillment, and ultimately joy. This journey has led me to you. This book can help you find wealth and abundance that you have never experienced previously. You can enjoy deeper and more meaningful relationships, and find emotional and spiritual health, that you may have only dreamed about. This book can help you allow yourself to be happy and enjoy success in your career, relationships, and personal life.

It has always frustrated me that self-development speakers or teachers say happiness is a choice. How does a person make that choice? You see, a choice implies a concrete answer and an outcome to that choice. If I choose to wear my red shirt, I put my red shirt on. If I choose to drive faster, I push the accelerator down. Choice has a cause and effect. So what do you do when you choose happiness? Can you just quit being unhappy? No, we all need choices that can be measured that ultimately lead to happiness. Happiness is not a choice; it is a series of choices that result in happiness. In this book you will see my journey to achieve happiness and the choices I believe lead a person to develop happiness from within. It does this by identifying thoughts and actions that you can implement in your life that inevitably will bring joy.

I cared for my beautiful wife who suffered with lupus for many years, had a home burn down, was widowed at thirty-four years old, was a single parent with three daughters under eight, remarried four years later, had a baby pass away at birth, survived a devastating divorce, had a once successful company go out of business, suffered bankruptcy, and struggled with intense depression. Life simply had become too hard, and I either needed to do something to find joy or I would be unable to continue. I personally have taken these steps in the book and they have given me a joy that I didn't know could exist. This happiness is with me despite the continued adversity that is in my life. I hope you can find the same peace and joy through the things that I have learned.

Chapter 2

Applying the Law of Attraction

As you will hear me say many times throughout this book, we are on this earth to feel joy and happiness. We do this through several ways, many of which are in this book: love, service, kindness, developing our talents, conquering fear, etc. When you are not feeling joy, you simply are not in harmony with those powerful elements. However, there is much more to it than that.

*"Ask and it shall be given you, seek and you shall find, knock and it shall be opened unto you."* *Mathew 7:7*

Many of you may have been introduced to and perhaps even studied the Law of Attraction. Entire books have been written on this subject alone, and it is essential to provide a brief discussion of this important principle in this book. The Law of Attraction has become very popular recently even though the concept has been around for centuries. In its most direct form, the Law of Attraction says that which is like unto itself is drawn to itself. Every thought radiates a vibration, if you will, and that vibration receives back a matching vibration.

Let me illustrate this with an example. For several years I worked in radio. At one time or another I did most everything one can do at a radio station. But what never ceased to amaze me was how what we were doing from a small building in downtown Salt Lake City was transmitted through a metal tower and received by people in their moving cars who were *expecting* to hear what we were saying. Our radio frequency was 97.1 FM. Someone who wanted to listen to sports radio 570 AM would not suddenly hear our station. Only those who desired to hear 97.1 and matched their radio to that same frequency were able to hear us. Putting it another way, people who wanted a specific type of programming adjusted their dial to get that program. They knew what they wanted and adjusted their dial to get it. Had that program not come through when they set their dial, they would have been shocked.

Now, in our technologically sophisticated world, we can explain the technology of radio signals in tremendous detail. However, someone from New England in the 1600s would think we were witches and likely have drowned us in a lake or burned us at the stake had we made such claims. Does the fact that those people centuries ago who didn't understand radio frequencies make the science any less real? No, the reality is that the science had always existed; it just took someone discovering and developing the technology to realize its benefits. Today we simply turn our station to 97.1 and expect that it is there.

In many ways we are like the Puritans of the 1600s when it comes to the Law of Attraction. Many people do not understand how it works and therefore label it as untrue, or in other words, witchcraft. That perception does not change the "science" or truth of the Law of Attraction; it simply alters their ability to recognize it and control its effect on their lives.

All of us at some time in our lives have been lying on the ground at night looking into the vast universe. Perhaps we were trying to identify constellations of stars, or simply taking in its beauty. It is always an awe-inspiring moment to imagine the depth of the sky and its distances that are measured in light-years. To think that our natural eyes are only seeing the smallest of fractions of the universe is virtually incomprehensible.

Rarely do we think about the universe going the other direction, that is, looking for the smallest of particles and waves that make up all things. When we do try and understand and "view" things on the subatomic level, or the quantum level, it can be equally as awe-inspiring as looking into space. But this is the place where we learn how the Law of Attraction works. This is where we see it as science rather than mysticism.

We are all used to the cause and effect of the

physical world. For example, if you strike a billiard ball with another ball, you can anticipate its reaction. It is based on angles that are consistent and part of the immutable laws that govern our physical world. These laws don't change and are the basis of Newtonian physics. In the quantum domain, things are much different. The existence of it is no less scientific and "real" as is the physical domain, but we are unable to detect it with our five senses. Just as you are not able to detect the furthest regions of the Milky Way galaxy, you are unable to detect the quantum world, which we are all part of.

Think back to your first science classes in school. We are taught that all objects are made up of very small units called molecules, which are in turn made up of even smaller units called atoms.

Your mind, thoughts, ego, and other parts that you typically think of as "you" are all part of the quantum domain. You can't see them, taste them, feel them, or hear them, but they are no less real than something you can detect with your senses. As you continue to drill down on the smallest of particles, you see that all things are moving continuously and are made of energy and information. Yes, even that desk in front of you is made of particles of energy and information and at its subatomic level is no more solid than a glass of water. Waves of energy are the core of all things. It is in those waves of energy that we find the Law of Attraction explained. We understand that energy has components of attraction. The involvement between protons and neutrons has a magnetic interrelationship. In the most basic of science classes, we would use magnets to explain the science of energy.

With this most basic of understanding, we can now see that the Law of Attraction is simply a scientific law that we can learn to use for our benefit or demise.

Often what I will hear from people is: *Why am I not getting the things I want in my life?* It is not because you don't want it enough. It is not because you are unworthy or do not deserve it enough. It is not because fate is against you. The reason you are not receiving the things you want in your life is because of one thing, and one thing only: you are on a different frequency than that which you desire. You are on the proverbial sports station but expect to hear Mariah Carey. No matter how long you stay there, you will never hear Mariah Carey.

Abundance and prosperity are always flowing to you; however, it is up to you to be in a state of allowing to receive the gifts. In other words, you are either in a state of allowing or resisting at all times. When we are allowing, we find tremendous blessings in our life. When we are resisting, we don't feel quite so blessed. The obvious question then would be: why in the world would we ever be in a state of resisting? The answer is simple. It is because we are unable to recognize it when we are in that condition. As you gain more understanding and experience, you will recognize that the more you *expect* an outcome to occur, the more likely it is to happen. Let me restate this in a different way: to the degree you expect good things and blessings to flow to you indicates the level of your state of allowing.

Now is the perfect time for you to begin to deliberately allow for the blessings of the Law of Attraction to flow to you. You may be in prison, divorcing, or in financial ruin; it does not matter. Regardless of your current condition, now is the best time to start your deliberate allowing of positive attraction. I live in the Salt Lake City, Utah, area. It is a wonderful place to live but I like to travel frequently to San Diego. I love the warm weather and the beautiful scenery of the ocean. When I drive to San Diego, I know that it is approximately 750 miles and takes me about ten hours to get there. Yes, I have a significant problem with speeding.

As I drive along the route through southern Utah in to Nevada, I begin to like the drive less and less. When I reach Death Valley in southeastern California, I wonder how anyone could have ever decided to inhabit the area. It is really my least favorite place on the planet. It is hot and ugly, no offense to those who live in Baker, California. Do you think at any time I say to myself, "This drive sucks; I am going to turn around and go home?" Of course not, but why is that? It is because I know that in the end I will be sitting on a beach enjoying one of the best places on earth. When I started on this trip, I didn't expect to get there instantaneously, nor did I expect to enjoy every moment of the journey. But I recognized my goal and knew that it would be realized. I just need to stay on course and keep moving forward.

Life and being in an allowing state of being is much like this journey I take to San Diego. You must know for a certainty where you are going to arrive and understand that there may be moments of difficulties, but they are only hiccups and cannot dissuade you from your journey. You never quit and turn around and go home. This level of expectation, or allowing, will engage the Law of Attraction and realize tremendous blessings for you.

Again, you are always in either of state of allowing or resistance. Practice being in a state of allowing to generate the positive gifts associated with the Law of Attraction. In order to "practice," you need to have a way to measure your progress. We have all been blessed with a barometer that measures our current attitude and actions and how they match with our desires. That barometer is our feelings. Many people who have only studied the Law of Attraction on the surface think that simply displaying pictures or words of affirmation on the wall are enough to engage the law. That is simply not true. You must feel to your core what you desire is coming or is, in fact, already here. It is feelings that engage the Law of Attraction, not wishes.

When someone asks you how you are doing, you almost always respond the same way regardless of how you are really feeling. "Fine, how are you?" However, now you need to start asking yourself that question and answering honestly and clearly. The more you are in a state of resistance, the more you will feel sadness, depression, and other negative emotions. When you are in a state of allowing, you will feel satisfaction, happiness, and other positive emotions. Use these feelings to assess your current congruency with the Law of Attraction. Don't use these feelings to dictate where you will be emotionally. For example, oftentimes depression can spiral out of control. It begins to feed on itself and a person becomes more and more depressed. Simply, his or her depression attracts further feelings of depression and can continue that state of being almost indefinitely. Rather than allow that to occur, recognize that you are depressed because you are not in harmony with your desires and what you are attracting. Start reassessing what you most desire and alter your expectations to match that desire. Depression and sadness will dissipate and be replaced with feelings of confidence and joy. That is when you know you are in harmony with the universal Law of Attraction.

I love golf. It has been part of my life since I was nine years old. I really was never very good at it, but I always loved the challenge it gave me. Over the years I have read many books on the subject, including thousands of pages on putting. There is one thing in all that I have read that has had a great impact on my golf, and in reality in my life generally. Jack Nicklaus in his book *Golf My Way* discussed the importance of "seeing" your golf shot before you hit the ball. See the ball fly off your club into the air and gently land exactly where you want it. Feel the excitement of the success of the shot. This visualization of the golf shot is used by virtually every professional golfer today. It is clear to these professional athletes that seeing and feeling the outcome of a shot before the shot occurs improves the likelihood of the shot's success dramatically.

Feeling the outcome of anything, not just golf shots, before doing it improves the likelihood of the success of that thing.

Now in life you will have times when you are going through "Death Valley." It is fine to recognize that is your current condition; just remember to focus on the outcome of your journey and the brief moments in the perilous desert will quickly fade. By engaging and being in a state of allowing rather than resistance, you will have the blessings of God flow to you like never before. Always be grateful for the blessings and use them to bless the lives of other people.

## How to Manifest Your Desires

Once you have an understanding of the Law of Attraction and its reality in your life, you are open to controlling it to obtain the wishes of your soul. Don't start picking out all the things you want in your life and "request" them to be given to you. The Law of Attraction isn't a proverbial Santa Claus. The list of things will come naturally to you as you assess your life and its meaning. But even before that you must understand the steps that can trigger the Law of

Attraction and help you realize your dreams.

First, you must honor your worthiness to receive that which you desire. For some reason many of the beliefs or religions of the day want you to feel unworthy and small, as if to suggest that believing you are nothing or as insignificant as a grain of sand somehow makes God more...godlike. The belief that you are small and unworthy only attracts smallness and unworthiness. No, you need to understand that within you is God and God's power created you. Is there any greater reason to think of yourself as worthy and powerful? You should even take it a step further. If God created you, and you literally have the power of God within you, should you not also have the power to create your desires? Of course, but they are predicated on rules of the divine. The first rule being that you must accept that you are worthy to attract your desires.

There is a myth that abundance of material things is incompatible with spirituality or the spirit of God. It is spoken of in the Bible when the parable of a rich man is taught. You may recall that it says a rich man is as likely to enter the kingdom of heaven as a camel is to travel through the eye of a needle. Many theologians foolishly interpret that to mean a rich man can't get to heaven. Look at the vastness of the universe and its infinite resources. Why would God create such a universe only to suggest that having such abundance is somehow evil? No, there is no intrinsic evil in desiring abundance. Be humble, be quiet in your desires, and make the use of your abundance to the benefit of all mankind, and you will celebrate God in your abundance, not denigrate him.

All that you need to attract the desires of your heart is within your spirit. The world teaches that you must be a workaholic, forgoing happiness today for that which you want tomorrow. It even suggests that you may have to trample on others or somehow conquer the world to receive what you want. There may even be supposed examples of such people you can point to. What you don't see is the misery and pain inside these people. Their abundance is not the abundance you are looking for. You are looking for abundance that flows to you because of the immutable laws of attraction bringing you joy and peace, and allowing you to share it with others. To find that abundance doesn't require you to neglect your family or your role as a parent, it does not require you to conquer others, it simply requires that you honor your worthiness to attract such desires and follow the principles of the Law of Attraction.

To feel this worthiness may require some work for you initially. From our births we are often taught that we are unworthy. A fundamental belief in Christianity is that we are all born with the cloak of sin and therefore are a flawed creation. You must realize that as a child of God your divinity is a given. Therefore, the desires of your heart that are derived in love and service are also of God. The desire to manifest those things in your life are simply manifestations of God. I would remind you that whenever you are feeling that you are not worthy to receive the blessings of God, tell yourself that all people are worthy to manifest their desires. The same divine energy that runs through them runs through you. In fact, your desires are the very tools that allow you to grow and experience the perfection of the universe and all that God has to offer.

Some who feel unworthy struggle with who they are. To truly accept your worthiness to manifest your desires you must accept who you are without complaint. Every extra pound, wrinkle, or scar on your being is there for a reason, a divine reason. Your body and mind as they are at this very moment are God's chosen vehicle for your spirit. That means you are perfect just as you are. Since my early twenties, my bald head has been the butt of many a joke. Baldness is an easy target. I hated that trait and even went so far as to wear a hairpiece for a time in an effort to rectify the physical error. I look back on that time now and laugh at my thinking. There is no flaw, there is no weakness. There are only differences that make each of us unique. Don't misunderstand, this understanding is not to excuse bad behavior and poor decision making. You should honor yourself by eating healthy and taking care of yourself. Simply, this understanding should help you abstain from the self-loathing thinking that we erroneously barrage upon ourselves. If your inner energy is focused on what you perceive is wrong with you, you will only continue to manifest inadequacy.

The beauty about self-acceptance is that it only requires a shift in your thinking, a simple change of consciousness. It is not a false attitude; it is a deeper understanding and a removal of the need to be accepted by others. In fact, by controlling one's ego and removing the need for approval from others, and by accepting ourselves as is; shame, guilt, and inadequacy dissipate, and you become aligned with the divine power.

A complete acceptance of yourself as you are now puts you in a position to expand and grow to enjoy even greater abundance. Always remember you are perfect just as you are at this very moment.

Another critical element that helps you honor your worthiness to manifest your desires is taking complete responsibility for every part of your life. The days of blaming ex-spouses, parents, former associates, and others for the negative things in your life are gone. Every good *and* bad thing in your life was chosen in some form by you. If you decide that others are to blame for the bad things that have happened to you, then you must also leave the good things that have happened in others' hands as well. Essentially you are then accepting that you have no control over your life. That simply is not the case. Even harmful events that have been forced upon us, in some way we allowed to occur. Accept that every facet of your life is your responsibility and you will be on your way to manifesting your greatest desires.

Byron Katie has written several books and is one of my favorite authors. She teaches a beautiful philosophy she calls "The Work." It essentially encourages each of us to accept the things that happen as what is suppose to occur and learn to embrace it. Rather than fighting against what you can't control, you accept what is, take responsibility for your life, and move on. By accepting responsibility for every area of our lives, we reduce stress from fighting against that which we cannot control, and we allow the positive desires of our heart fertile ground in which to grow.

With the acceptance of responsibility for all that happens in your life, particularly the bad, you must also make a commitment to not accept guilt, in any form, to accompany that acceptance. Guilt is an unproductive emotion, heaped upon us from a misunderstanding of the divine. God has no desire to see you feel guilty and ashamed. It is fine to feel regret and learn from one's past mistakes. But it is imperative to understand that nothing in your past can dictate any action in the future. The past is like the wake of a boat. It certainly was caused by that boat, but it has no bearing on where that boat chooses to go. Remaining in a state of guilt and self-reproach simply stalls forward progress. Accept the past and your responsibility in it, learn from those events, and take corrective action to not repeat the mistakes. That is both an intellectually and spiritually sound response. Nowhere in that thinking does guilt play a role, and it shouldn't. Persistent feelings of guilt will prevent you from manifesting your desires. When you feel bad, you are not aligned with divinity and attracting that which is good is impossible.

Part of feeling worthy to attract your heart's desire will come when you are living an authentic life.

Living an authentic life means your thoughts, desires, and behavior are all in harmony with each other. If at anytime you are incongruent with any of these three areas, you are living an inauthentic life, which is incompatible with manifesting your desires. Your feelings are your barometer as to how authentic you are living your life. Feelings of uneasiness are always present when conflict between your thoughts, desires, and behavior occurs. Start becoming aware of even the slightest ripple in the change of your feelings and you will become highly sensitive to living an authentic life. This will require complete and utter honesty with yourself at all times. It's not an easy task and certainly a lifelong pursuit. But continued effort in this will bring you inner peace because all the areas of your life will be in harmony.

Perhaps the best way to align the areas of your life and live authentically is to root all of these things in the pursuit of love for yourself, others, and in fact, all things. If you accept that all of your behaviors toward yourself and others should be based in love, you will find forgiveness easier to offer to family members, coworkers, and others who cross your path. You will find yourself less likely to respond to negative things with anger and anxiety. The necessity for winning will subside as you revel in the success of others. Strive for love and you will find the natural occurrence of living authentically apparent in your life. With that harmony between thoughts, desires, and behavior comes your alignment with divinity and further ability to attract your heart's desires.

There is really no greater power in heaven or on earth than unconditional love.

Once you have committed to attracting your desires into your life, it is time to let go and let the universe do the heavy lifting. It does you no good to continually barrage heaven with your desires. As the great author Dr. Wayne Dyer says, "God is not a vending machine." If you put in enough coins (prayers), out comes your desires. God has your best interests at heart, and that which you desire is being furiously developed in the unseen background. It is your responsibility to allow that development and to detach yourself from the process and the expectations of the outcome. It will show up when the time is right. With that said, it is very appropriate to frequently feel the gratitude for the outcome, even before that outcome has occurred. It is also very appropriate to visit the feelings that you will possess having received your heart's desires, again even before they have arrived. For example, if your desire is financial, it is very appropriate to see yourself enjoying the abundance that the money provides. Allow yourself to feel the joy that helping a friend in need will realize as you share that abundance. Feeling the outcome is the key to the Law of Attraction, not wishing for the outcome. Let me reiterate that these are private matters. Keep these desires and feelings to yourself and treat them as sacred *currency,* if you will.

With the certainty of the outcome will come the

needed patience I speak of. It just seems easier when you know that all is being taken care of and is on its way. There is no looking around the corner to see if that "thing" that you want is here. You simply are at ease knowing that it will get here when it gets here.

Doubt is the enemy of manifesting your desires. For whatever reason, there is a natural inclination to doubt. We often hear it in people's expressions: "I never win anything," or "if I didn't have bad luck, I would have no luck at all." Fight doubt by using positive affirmations or other methods to be strong in your commitment to manifest your desires. If doubt begins to creep in, simply recognize that it has entered your mental stage and quickly ask it to leave. You are in control and simply recognizing doubt's presence will allow you to control its exit as well.

Now it is time to be on the lookout for the manifestations of your desires. Keep in mind they may show up different than your rational mind envisioned. That is why visualizing the feelings you may have rather than the things you may possess is so important. You may think that a million dollars will help you feel secure and stable. God is focused on helping you feel secure and stable; whether it is a million bucks or not really doesn't matter, he will decide. But rest assured, if you do the things discussed here, you will feel secure and stable. The outcome will occur; it just may arrive in a different manner than you anticipate. Just remember to be sensitive and recognize when the manifestation of your desires arrives and give continuous gratitude and humble acceptance of it.

The Law of Attraction is a beautiful understanding of the interrelationship between the physical and spiritual. By learning how it works and placing godlike attributes in your life, you will indeed be able to attract the most precious of your heart's desires. Whether it is the love of a partner, overcoming sickness, financial rewards, or any other positive outcome, you can manifest it in your life. Begin now to guide the Law of Attraction in your life and you will certainly find joy, even during times of adversity.

Chapter 3

# The Hardest Person to Love

We have all traveled different paths in life and have all experienced, to some degree, abuse at the hands of others. Many of us have experienced tremendous trauma, including sexual and child abuse. It simply is a tragedy of the highest order. However, no one has inflicted more damage on you than yourself. Let me repeat this! You have said and done more to harm yourself than any other person. It is estimated that we have approximately sixty thousand thoughts a day. What is most interesting is that we have virtually the same thoughts each and every day. How many of those thoughts each day have included looking in the mirror and saying you are fat, ugly, or stupid? How many times have you said you hate yourself? Have you ever wished you were dead? It may not even be that strong. You may look at yourself and just think, "Ugh!" Thousands upon thousands of times every one of us has said such hurtful things. Things we would never say to another person we say routinely to ourselves. Each word slowly chips away at our confidence, our hope, and or love, ultimately leading to a life of unhappiness and unfulfilled dreams.

It is time to start changing that destructive behavior.

When we are young children, we are full of love. We haven't yet bought into the perception of the world on what is pretty or ugly, smart or stupid, good or bad. We didn't look at someone with judgment. We simply loved. What is pretty? Ask any male teenager and he is likely to say a tall, 115-pound blonde woman. Where did he get that judgment? As a small child everyone was beautiful. Slowly we were taught what was pretty in society's opinion. As we grew we were indoctrinated into these norms. We were taught prejudice, judgment, and hatred. Finally, after adopting these doctrines, we became the teachers (parents), not deliberately misleading anyone, but because we now believed those things taught to us were true, we shared them with those we loved. This includes the self-abuse we thrust upon ourselves all of our lives. The perceptions that we have of the world work like viruses and spread from person to person, developing and multiplying until they become accepted as societal norms.

Over the last several years, the Law of Attraction has become the new, vogue, positive attitude adjustment belief. People have adopted this belief and committed to making changes in their lives to begin "attracting" abundance. This desire to adopt the Law of Attraction is admirable but nearly impossible to achieve unless we go to the source of our feelings. Why were we attracting negativity and lack of abundance previously? The answer is that we were taught false and negative beliefs from our earliest years as truths and correct principles, and we internalized the false perceptions. They must be changed to begin attracting the wonderful things this life has to offer. At this point, it is important to state that rarely are the "wonderful things" in this life related to money. Money is a worthy goal but has much more power in the Law of Attraction when its intent is to serve others. That is where true joy and fulfillment happen. Service!

After becoming aware that our thinking of the past was only our perceptions and can be changed, we are in a position to make that change. It simply isn't pasting pictures of things we want on a board and hanging them on our wall. That may be helpful, but our internal thinking must be changed. We must *feel* the positive thoughts as part of us. That *feeling* is when the Law of Attraction becomes engaged.

If you are ready, I will show you how to begin making that change.

Thought awareness leads to change. Your mind works so quickly that you are not even aware of the negative flow of ideas that flood your mind, damaging your life and happiness. Therefore you must train your mind to automatically replace the negative ideas with positive thoughts. Initially you will need to do this deliberately, but slowly your mind will adopt the positive thoughts and immediately replace the negative thoughts with a positive thought on its own.

Remember, you were originally built to feel unconditional love and happiness. Your mind will quickly adapt back to these beliefs because it is a natural condition. In the book of John in the New Testament, it says "God is love." You are part of God; he created you to be loving, kind, and to feel joy. This is the condition God wants you in.

It was always frustrating to me that people would say, change your thoughts and it will change your life. I accept that premise. But changing my thoughts consistently felt nearly impossible. I would be positive for days or even weeks at a time, but slowly old habits would creep in. Next thing I knew I was back where I started: negative thoughts attracting further conditions of negativity.

Finally, I was able to overcome that cycle. I memorized a positive statement that I would replay every time I recognized my mind perpetuating negativity. I know I just lost half the people reading this with a sigh of...negativity! Let me be clear. No strategy is easier and has more significant results than positive statements of affirmation. I heard about this process about thirty years ago. It took all those years for me to finally be humble enough to give it a try. Don't make the same mistake I made by dismissing it based on its simplicity. There are two reasons to use positive affirmation statements. First, to be able to control your thoughts and limit negativity. This is where I find them most useful. Second, to engage the Law of Attraction. This is only useful if you are able to internalize the statement as a feeling. In this chapter we are primarily using positive affirmations to help us control our thoughts and reduce negativity. Controlling negative thoughts ultimately leads to adopting these statements as beliefs or "feelings." Virtually every successful legendary author in personal development has taught the powerful principal of positive affirmations. There is a reason; it works beyond what you can imagine.

Here is the statement I use. I call it my Cornerstone Statement:

*I am worthy of unlimited abundance and prosperity, regardless of the life experiences of the past. I am a masterpiece of God. Perfect! Just as I am now at this very moment. I will only reinforce and contemplate images that are in harmony with this vision.*

Every time a negative thought would come into my mind I would replay this statement. Rather quickly I began to hear this positive statement played in my mind whenever my inner voice would say something negative. Now, instead of hearing, "You are fat!" I hear "I am a masterpiece of God. Perfect! Just as I am now at this very moment." If I hear, "I am a failure!" it is immediately replaced by, "I am worthy of unlimited abundance and prosperity." I now hear these positive, enlightened messages many times a day. Imagine the change in my self-image. Imagine the change in what I attract.

Why do I call it my Cornerstone? The cornerstone is the first stone set in a building upon which all other stones are built. If this first stone is done wrong, everything else after that is also wrong. This statement is the first statement to get my mind in a place where I can be blessed with a life of joy. Without this, all other efforts can be ineffective.

Let's break down the Cornerstone Statement.

### *I am worthy*

For me this was the hardest part of the Cornerstone to internalize. In our society we are taught that true humility is a virtue, which it is, but then we define it poorly. Society, particularly religions, look at "we are nothing, we are as dust" as a deeper level of humility. In fact, humility is a natural response to developing one's true godlike nature. The kinder, more forgiving, more loving you are, the virtue of humility is inevitably present. Demeaning oneself is simply a fake and misdirected attempt at being seen as humble. It is a wolf in sheep's clothing.

You are worthy of everything God can and will give you. You are worthy because you are part of and created by God.

### *I am worthy **of unlimited abundance and prosperity,***

Unlimited abundance and prosperity are defined differently by all of us. Notice I didn't put "unlimited wealth." That may be part of the equation for you, but I must caution you, selfishness is a quick way to short-circuit the power of positive attraction. Selfishness will attract selfishness. With that said, money is a wonderful way to impact many lives. It can bring opportunities to you and others in ways that are not possible without it. This is a positive desire.

I believe abundance is everything I need to effectively develop my passions and talents. God gives us these talents and passions to be developed, not to be blocked and stifled. Prosperity is growth in all that is good in your life. That may be deeper friendships, closer connections to family, or more success in the things that are meaningful in your life.

### *I am worthy of unlimited abundance and prosperity, **regardless of the life experiences of the past.***

You have heard many times that past performance is the best indicator of future success. The very fact that when you apply for a job you are asked for a resume underscores that point. I am here to tell you that is only true for those who don't understand the principles of spiritual and emotional growth. It is only true for those who don't understand how changing their thoughts can alter the things that are attracted to their lives. You are not that person. The fact that you are holding this book is because change has been attracted to your life. The past is important, regardless of what has occurred, because it has made you what you are today. The problem is when you accept that failures of the past result in failures in the future. You are not your past; in fact, you are not your future. You are simply what you are at this very moment. The abundance and prosperity of the future is in no way connected to the life experiences of the past. Which leads us to the next positive phrase in the Cornerstone Statement.

*I am worthy of unlimited abundance and prosperity, regardless of the life experiences of the past.* **I am a masterpiece of God. Perfect! Just as I am now at this very moment.**

My point here is not to convince you there is a God. Nor do I desire to define who or what God is to you. That is a personal matter for each of us to assess on our own. What I do ask of you is to recognize there is an order to our universe. Something keeps all of the universe in an undeniable harmony, of which you are a part. Some call it Source Energy, some Allah, Christ, Buddha, or simply "a higher power." Whatever your belief, I am asking you to recognize that God made you the way you are because that is what he wanted for you at this moment. It is his perfect order. In that belief you must then recognize the perfection of his creation of all things. That means, right now at this moment, you are exactly where God wants you. That doesn't mean that you are destined to be in the same place tomorrow or ten years from now. In fact, through growth by your choice, I hope you won't be. Simply, you are where God wants you now. You are his masterpiece! Perfect! Just as you are now at this very moment. Embrace that!

*I am worthy of unlimited abundance and prosperity,*
*regardless of the life experiences of the past.*
*I am a masterpiece of God. Perfect! Just as I am now at this very moment.*
***I will only reinforce and contemplate images***
***that are in harmony with this vision.***

In the last phrase of the Cornerstone Statement I reiterate that I will only allow positive images to thrive in my mind. This does not mean negative thoughts will not show up. They will! The key is whether you reinforce them by allowing supportive negative thoughts to enter.

One night at about midnight, my daughter Jamie came running into my bedroom. "Dad, Dad," she said, "there is something scratching at the garage door." We have an adjoining garage that has a door into the house. I looked around and both of our dogs were in the house. My next thought was that Jamie was probably watching a scary movie that had gotten to her a bit. I slowly dragged myself out of bed and walked into the family room where the entrance to the garage was. I slowly grabbed the doorknob while Jamie was sheltered behind me, peering over my shoulder. I heard the noise. *Scratch, scratch, scratch.* It didn't sound like a big dog. My first thought at that point was that a small neighbor dog must have snuck through the open door when we were driving in and got stuck in there. That worried me because I had no idea what to expect from the dog. Would it be angry and hungry? I slowly opened the door and looked into the dark garage. It took a moment for my eyes to adjust to the figure that was standing there in the blackness, and just then my daughter yelled, "Skunk!" as the little black-and-white creature stuck his tail in the air and pointed his posterior directly at us. I squealed like a teenage schoolgirl and slammed the door just in the nick of time to avoid the skunk's odiferous delivery. It took us three days to finally get that skunk out of my garage. Can you imagine the damage had he come into the house?

Why do I tell you such a story? I can't think of a better metaphor for a negative thought than a skunk. It can do you no harm unless you let it in; then it can wreak havoc and be very difficult to remove. Even after it's gone, you are going to suffer with the horrible smell it left behind. The unfortunate thing is that all too often the garage door to our mind doesn't exist. There really is nothing there to stop the negative thought from coming in. Once into your mind the painful results grow and cause tremendous damage. Even if you finally get that thought out of your mind, there is oftentimes a residue left behind that lingers for some time after. It is so much better to keep the skunk in the garage and never open the door. That is what the Cornerstone Statement does.

In the Cornerstone you commit to only reinforce and contemplate images that support unlimited abundance and prosperity, and your wonder as God's creation. When a negative thought enters your mind, it will begin to be immediately replaced by the positive statements directed by the Cornerstone. Simply, the garage door is slammed in its face. Negativity will ultimately only have fleeting moments of "air time" in your mind. For me it is most often when I'm driving. If people would just use their blinkers!

Loving yourself is critical to finding joy. You must be able to understand that in all the wrinkles, extra weight, baldness, and foolishness and mistakes made, is something glorious. That something is you and it is God's greatest creation. Focusing on what you believe to be weakness is not in harmony with divinity and will only reinforce unhappiness. By learning to control your thoughts, you will begin to see your own majesty and the beauty of all creation. You will begin to love all of you. You will begin to find joy.

# Chapter 4

# You are a Domino

I was watching this video recently that showed the most incredible domino progression. We have all seen things like this. One domino falls over and triggers thousands of other dominoes to fall. This video impacted me perhaps because of the gradual increase of things that moved from that single motion. The tipping over of a domino began involving the movement of other objects. At one point a piano is moved and a car is put in motion, all because a single domino fell. Energy has a way of building, and as it builds, more and more reactions occur.

Life is motion. Everything we do, even every thought we have, ripples through the universe like the domino. A small thing may trigger many things, leading to something huge. No matter what we choose to do, it triggers reactions leading to other reactions, leading to other reactions, and so on, and so forth. I believe that an action that starts out positive builds positive energy and continues affecting the universe positively. The same can be said for negative energy.

Let me introduce you to a domino.

Mrs. Dilworth from Paris, Idaho, completely changed my life, and to this day she has no idea. When I was in my early twenties I was really hurting financially. I happened to walk into the music store of my old drum teacher. This was a great store; it was in an old beat-up building that had been falling apart for probably forty years. It was recognized as one of the great local music stores in Salt Lake City. I just liked going in there to look at new instruments. One of the employees was a few years older than me and looked exactly like the eighties hair band rocker. He was the drummer for a band that was playing a gig that night in Montpelier, Idaho, a rural town that you would really not have any reason to go to if you weren't a rancher...or a mediocre rock band. The drummer had a conflict and he wanted someone to sit in with the band tonight. Now I hadn't played the drums for a few years, and frankly, I wasn't very good when I was playing. He assured me that it was just a quiet lounge where I wouldn't have to play anything but a simple beat. He said, "Just play quiet enough and no one will even know you are there."

He was lying.

I really needed the couple hundred bucks this gig would pay, so I agreed to go. His band picked me up and we headed to Montpelier, about three hours away. I was packed in a small, tattered car that was jammed with instruments and amplifiers. It was a cold day, too early to be called spring but not cold enough to feel like winter. Of course, I didn't take a coat. When we pulled into town, we parked at an old cowboy bar located on Main Street. This was not a quiet lounge. We were late, so we hurried and set up. There wasn't going to be any practicing and I didn't know any of the songs on the song list. Have you ever been to a cowboy bar in cowboy country? It is loud and alcohol fuels a very rough crowd.

Well, it became apparent quickly that I was playing with a rock band. The music was loud, fast, and unrecognizable. Remember, I had never been a good drummer and I thought I would be playing a simple four/four beat, and certainly no drum fills. Well, I was terrible and the band members kept giving me "you suck" stares followed by unpleasant hand signals. I was in over my head; they knew it and I knew it. Within about three songs I was kicked out of the band. They pulled a completely drunk cowboy out of the audience and he played the drums like I wished I could have. I was embarrassed and upset and wished so badly I had driven there in my own car. But I hadn't, so I was stuck there. What made it more painful was that it was a two-night gig. That was Friday night; they also were booked to play on Saturday night. I was stuck there. Little did I know the painful experience was just beginning.

After a couple hour set, the bar owner took us to the apartment where we were going to sleep. It looked like the worst room in a low-income brothel. It had no beds and the window glass was broken, allowing the thirty-degree night air free access to our room. I slept on that filthy floor that night with a small blanket that allowed me to either cover my feet or my body, but not both. I froze and was miserable all night long.

When I awoke the next morning, I had had enough of Montpelier, the rock band, and anything associated with it. I found an old, cardboard, twelve-pack beer box, wrote "Salt Lake City or Bust" on one side, and walked out to the highway. I was ready to catch a ride with anyone to anywhere to get out of there. It was pretty cold that day, probably in the low forties, and I didn't have a coat. I was freezing but I stood at that spot just outside of town with my thumb outstretched, praying for someone to get me the heck out of there. I stood there for nearly ten hours and no one stopped. I didn't know what to do. The sun was starting to set and I knew that I couldn't stand out there when it got dark. I didn't have the money for a motel room, and the thought of going back to the cowboy bar was unbearable.

This is when I met Mrs. Dilworth. She stopped in front of me in a station wagon that had to be from the early seventies. It looked like it had two hundred thousand miles on it. With her were her three children. She explained to me that she had passed me earlier and asked her children, "What would we do if that were Jesus?" The children piped in with kind actions. "We would help him"; another said, "We would feed him." As she explained this to me, she invited me to get in her car and she would make me a nice dinner. I was concerned because she lived in a town several miles from Montpelier. If I accepted her invitation, I would be in a smaller town, if that was possible, with nowhere to stay on a dark, cold night without a coat. But the thought of staying with the band felt worse, so I got in her car. Imagine a woman with three very small children pulling over to pick up a male hitchhiker and offering to take him to her home for dinner. To this day, just that alone is stunning to me, but my story had just begun.

I learned that Mrs. Dilworth was married, but her husband was unable to find work in rural Idaho and had moved to Washington for a job. She was left to care for the children, the home, and several farm animals. Additionally, she was absolutely broke and was barely surviving financially. She started cooking and made a lovely dinner that would usually be reserved for holidays. It was wonderful. I hadn't eaten at all that day and that may be one of the best meals I had ever eaten. After the meal had concluded, I knew that it was time for me to leave. It was now around 8:30 p.m. and pitch black outside. As I prepared to leave, she said to her children, "Now if this were Jesus, what would we do? Would we just feed him? No, we would drive him to Salt Lake City." It has been nearly thirty years since that day and I still remember the feeling that gave me. This person didn't have nearly enough money to be feeding me and certainly didn't have money to take me all the way to Salt Lake City. But her belief that helping someone in time of need was equivalent to helping Jesus compelled her to do otherwise. That is a person of faith.

She gathered the children, called a neighbor to help feed her animals the next day, and we were off to Salt Lake. It was nearly midnight when we arrived at my apartment. I was exhausted by one of the longest two days of my life. I thanked her for her kindness, and she left to go stay at a family member's house just outside of Salt Lake.

I staggered to my apartment door fiddling with my keys, trying to get my apartment door key out. The porch light wasn't on and I couldn't see, so I methodically went through my keys hoping one of them would fit in the lock. I would slide one in the key hole, twist, and move on to the next key until I finally had the right one. As I swung open the door, my roommate was standing there with a gun pointed straight at my head. He was ready to shoot when I yelled, "It's me, it's me, it's me." You see, he knew that I was supposed to be in Idaho until Sunday afternoon. It was Saturday night. As I was shaking the doorknob to get in the apartment, he thought someone was breaking in. At that point I wouldn't have minded him pulling the trigger and putting me out of my misery.

If the story were to end there, it would be an amazing story of kindness extended to me by a stranger. But it doesn't end there. Early the next morning I decided to attend church. I wasn't planning on going because I was supposed to be in Idaho. I considered sleeping in and not worrying about attending. The previous two days had been exhausting. However, I felt compelled to get up early and attend the meeting.

While sitting in a Sunday school classroom, I saw the most beautiful woman I had ever seen. She was visiting from California. I don't know if she knew that I was completely attracted to her, but in between church meetings she walked up to me, introduced herself, and asked me for directions to another church sermon later that night. I have never been real good at knowing women and when they are interested in me. To this day, I can't read a woman. So after she continued to hint that she wanted me to ask her out, I finally got the message. That night, I learned that she was only there for a few days, and had I not come home from Idaho early, I would have never met my lovely wife and the mother of my three beautiful daughters. Had Mrs. Dilworth not asked her children what Jesus would do if he saw a man on the side of the road, and acted upon it, I would have never met my beloved Kameo. That single decision changed my life forever. Mrs. Dilworth was a domino in my life. We are all dominos in many lives.

The goal of this book is to help you develop your life to be fulfilled and joyous in times of adversity. Loving others is one of the best ways to find that joy. No other subject has been explored, written, or sung about more than love of others. Take that as a sign of its importance.

Love is not a passive emotion. As with Mrs. Dilworth, love may require sacrifice and commitment. Regardless of the capacity it is in, it requires us to give more than we receive. In some cases we give love only to have it rebuffed. But give it we must. It does not matter how our love is received, only that it was given.

Obviously learning to love others is a lifelong pursuit, and your success with it will ebb and flow. It is simple to love those who love you. It is even easy to love those who like you. The challenge is learning to love those who have offended you or even hurt you. I need a system to try and help me develop love for the people who are difficult to love. I do this by adopting what I call the Circle of Love.

Whether it is toward someone frequently in your life or someone who simply passes through your world, the further you go in the Circle of Love, the more love flows from you, and the happier and more fulfilled your life will be. Love generates happiness in both the giver and receiver.

Remember, the Circle of Love is a great way to help you develop love *for those you find difficult to love.*

Your are a Domino

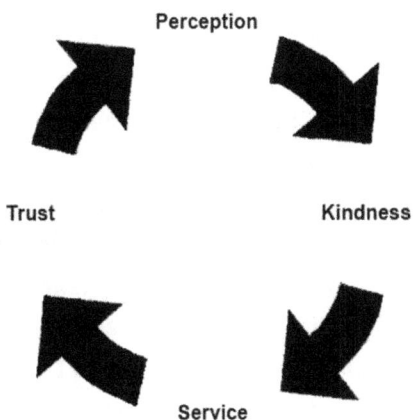

Perception

Trust                                    Kindness

Service

**Circle of Love**

## Step 1 – Perception

The first step is to not take the actions or words of another person too seriously. Oftentimes misunderstandings occur and then are followed up with words of anger, which are escalated by more words of anger, ultimately leaving two people believing that the other person is a jerk. Really, it all started with you accepting what another person said as reality when, truthfully, anything another person says to you is simply his perception only. He may tell you that you are wrong, but are you? You may or may not be wrong; that is simply his perception of you. His perception only matters if you allow it to matter. Imagine simply rebuffing someone's negative comments as of no importance to you. You don't get angry, and more

49

importantly, you don't accept his perception as true. You simply allow him his belief and you move on.

Equally of importance is to realize that when someone tells you that you are a genius, this too is a perception. It is no more true than when someone tells you something negative about yourself. But in the spirit of trying to love a person, it is much easier to love someone who doesn't like you if you neither accept nor reject their thoughts, and set them aside simply as their perception. That allows you to move on to the next step of Kindness, because anger hasn't escalated in the Perception stage. If anger does accelerate in this stage, the relationship with that person is doomed to fail, and that negative energy will reduce the joy in your life.

**Step 2 – Kindness**

Keep in mind that each step in the Circle of Love is meant to deepen love toward a person, which enhances your happiness. Once you are able to accept a person, regardless of their actions towards you, you are in a position to show kindness. Look for an opportunity to show this person some sign of kindness. It may simply be complimenting a person's outfit, telling her you like her smile, or thanking her for something. I realize this seems a little trite, but it starts to build in you a habit of being proactively kind despite what other people are doing. Do this as many times as you need to until you are comfortable moving to the next step.

## Step 3 – Service

By now you should start feeling some connection with a person. That person may now be showing you some kindness as well, and showing parts of his or her personality you didn't know existed. If this is not happening, you may really never get beyond "Step 2 – Kindness" with that person but keep trying. The deeper you can take this person in the Circle of Love, the more joy you will find in your life. Service is not kindness; it is reaching out and doing something you see this person needs that requires time and effort. It requires sacrifice from you. Mrs. Dilworth served me, which forced a significant sacrifice from her. It disrupted her children's and her own life, which is what service needs to do to be effective.

## Step 4 – Trust

To truly have love for someone demands that you be vulnerable. Think about it, in every deep relationship you have, or have had, the other person has known things about you that "no one else knows." This trust in the other person is a tremendously bonding experience, and if reciprocated can lead to a lifelong relationship experienced only a few times in a person's life. By allowing oneself to be vulnerable, one is taking a greater risk. Just like investing in stocks, the greater the risk, the greater return. You can put your money under your mattress and never risk losing any of it, or you can invest it wisely and potentially grow it, but have the chance of losing it. In matters of love, if you never allow yourself to take a risk and allow for the chance to be betrayed by another, you will really never have deep relationships. This is true in both romantic and platonic relationships.

As we know, betrayal in such a relationship is devastating; but always remember we heal, and the depth of love that trusting bond generates is well worth the loss and pain felt by some of those relationships.

I have been blessed in my life to have a handful of lifelong friends. These friendships go back decades and will continue for the duration of my life. In one case a friend has known me every day of my life, and either I will be speaking at his funeral or he will be speaking at mine. I have a very different relationship with each of these friends, but in every case they know very personal things about me. Things that may be embarrassing, painful, or misunderstood if other people knew them. But in their hands, it has allowed them to give me love and support that only they can give. By the way, I know personal things about them also.

It is obvious that a book that is providing guidance on how to find happiness during times of adversity would include a chapter on loving others. We are taught in virtually every religious text, the "golden rule." Love thy neighbor as thyself. Or in other words, treat others as you would have them treat you. Notice it doesn't say treat others as they treat you but "as you would have them treat you." In my life I have found that by using the incremental steps of the Circle of Love, I can be a more loving person to others, particularly those who may have wronged me or those who have negative feelings for me. Instead of telling myself I need to "love them," I can tell myself that they have their own perception of me, and I am going to do something kind for them. After I have done something kind, I can encourage myself to do service for them. Remember, with each step around the Circle of Love, and with each person in it, your life will become increasingly filled with joy.

You are a domino in other people's lives, regardless of whether you want to be or not. The decision you need to make is what type of domino you wish to be. If you truly want to be happy, be a domino like Mrs. Dilworth.

Chapter 5

# The Power of Passion

This chapter may be the single most influential contributor to your personal happiness than anything else written in this book. We have always known that each of us is truly one of a kind. Our face, our personality, our fingerprints...all one of a kind. Additionally, we all have a unique mix of things that we are passionate about. It may be music, art, charity work, science, or a host of other things. There are even those who are passionate about math. I know, that's hard to believe. The variety of things you are passionate about is as unique as your fingerprints.

For as long as man has inhabited earth we have watched birds soar and wanted to be one of them. I remember when I took my first solo flight in a Cessna 152 as a private pilot. Looking down the thousands of feet, I got a sense of what a bird must feel like. There is a sense of freedom that is hard to find any other way.

But there is a group of extreme athletes who have taken flight to an entirely new level. They are base jumpers on steroids and are wearing "wingsuits." These seemingly insane people climb high atop a sheer cliff thousands of feet above the ground. They throw themselves off these cliffs, free falling toward the ground. Wingsuits are designed to catch air and provide lift to the jumper. This incredible suit has webbing between the body and arms and legs. As the speed of the fall increases, the suit begins to catch air. As a result, it gives lift and lengthens the time that a person can stay in flight. This while going speeds in excess of 140 miles per hour and just feet from the jagged rocks of the cliff. At the last possible moment, the jumper pulls the rip cord and a parachute inflates bringing him or her safely to the ground.

It is an incredible sight to see a person torpedo toward the ground at such an extreme speed and then fly. As you can imagine, this hobby is unbelievably dangerous and the slightest mistake is punished by death. We should ask ourselves why anyone would risk his or her life for a brief moment of exhilaration. How could anyone justify that risk with the potential outcome? The answer is clear if you understand passion and how it supercharges the joy in a person's life. These people aren't just having several seconds of exhilaration. It encompasses their life. Every moment they spend planning, saving money, and hiking a mountain is filled with joy because it is developing their passion for flying. Now most of us don't have passions that are quite so physically challenging and risky. But all of us have passions that are spiritually, physically, and emotionally exhilarating, and the risk is not in pursuing the passion, it is in neglecting it.

Passions are placed inside of each of us by divinity. You could say that your passions are the signature of God within you. Obviously we are not referring to passions that are tied to romance and infatuation. Rather, we understand that passions are those things that bring enthusiasm to your life. The very thought of being involved in the things you are passionate about immediately brings a sense of joy. Imagine that, simply thinking about what you are passionate about generates happiness. When you actually participate in and develop those passions, you can generate a life that is joyful in every way. Remember, God wants you to live a fulfilled and happy life; however, it is up to you to recognize the gifts given you and develop those passions. To ignore them, which most of us do, is to ensure limited happiness. If we ignore them long enough, they will simply disappear.

I had suppressed the things I was passionate about for many years. Rather I opted to take the safe road and do the things that were expected of me, by working at a certain type of job, being a certain kind of man, and not recognizing the things inside of me waiting to be explored and developed. When I finally understood the power of passions and what it meant to embrace them, my life changed. Happiness became not only likely but inevitable.

When I first asked myself what my passions were, the first thought that came to my mind was helping others. Now that is an odd passion and certainly not something I could define well and could develop. At least that is what I thought. How do I like to help others? Should I quit my job in finance and work for a nonprofit organization? That didn't feel exactly right. I even considered joining the Peace Corps. Again, that just didn't resonate with me. I decided to analyze the other areas that I was passionate about. Writing, public speaking, and spirituality quickly became the primary passions I had. As I looked at these other areas that I was passionate about, they all just seemed to become a synergistic mix. What could I do that developed all of these passions? This led to my becoming a professional speaker and author focusing on the development of happiness in other people's lives. All of these fell under the umbrella of helping others.

Additionally, music and art were passions of mine. It became clear to me as I analyzed my mix of passions that they needed some prioritization. You cannot make everything you are passionate about a career. In fact, you may not be able to make anything you are passionate about a career. That will be up to you. But it is absolutely critical for you to recognize your passions and somehow incorporate them into your life, if only for a brief moment every day. This is a critical step in prolonged happiness. I can't play guitar as regularly as I would like, but I feel a responsibility to continue to develop that skill. It is a passion of mine.

When I play, it makes me happy.

When assessing your own passions, I want you to enlarge your vision. By that I mean I want you to spend time with your passions, considering different ways that you might develop them. Initially my thoughts of being passionate about helping others had limited application. I figured it primarily meant I would do charity work when I could put it into my busy schedule. That was not terribly meaningful to me. By enlarging my vision, I soon began to understand the potential of this passion. Initially you may not see the potential of your passions. But you will if you let them build and grow within you.

Jesus teaches the parable of talents. There are various interpretations of this parable, but for our purposes, we will keep it simple. A talent was a unit of measurement, usually associated with silver as a currency. However, it is often used literally to define the gifts a person has received from God. In the parable a master gives three servants five, two, and one talent respectively for which they were responsible. After being gone for a significant time, the master returns and asks the servants for an accounting of what has become of the talents entrusted to them. The first two servants had doubled the amount given them and were rewarded equally by the master. "Well done, my faithful servant, thou has been faithful over a few things; I will make thee the ruler of many things." The final servant had buried his talent, afraid that if he did anything with it, he might lose it. The master was angry with him. He had been given something and had done nothing to develop it further. The master rebuked him and told him he was a wicked and slothful servant. He took his single talent and gave it to the servant with ten talents.

We all have been given gifts that we carry inside of us. Whether we have five gifts or one gift, it is incumbent on all of us to maximize that gift. By doing so, we have done that which will make our lives fulfilled and meaningful. By doing nothing, we ultimately lose even that which we have.

The great spiritual leader Lao Tsu taught, "Knowing others is wisdom, knowing yourself is enlightenment." By being aware and developing your passions, you will know yourself.

One of my dreams as a young person was to be a professional musician, a rock star, if you will. For some reason I was embarrassed to share that with anyone and kept the secret to myself. After all, who was I to dream so big? I had tremendous passion for playing the piano in my teenage years but again kept this mostly a secret. My friends and even my parents really had no idea of my skill level at the piano. During my teenage years, on weekday evenings I would borrow the keys to my church and go play the baby grand in the chapel. There was something very special about playing in the dimly lit, large room that resonated with me.

I met and became very good friends with a nineteen-year-old named John. I mentioned to him in passing that I played the piano, but he had never heard me play. John was responsible for putting together a

Christmas program and asked me to perform. He had no idea what he was asking. I had never performed a piano solo in front of anyone ever! Putting my fear and self-doubt aside, I accepted.

When the day came for me to perform, I got a tremendous headache out of sheer terror. I could barely function. That actually may have been a blessing because I was so sick that I just wanted it to be over. I walked up on the stage, took a deep breath, and played and sang very well. It was a wonderful, pivotal moment for me. I was good! People kept coming up to me and telling how great they thought I was. To a young person with low self-esteem in this area, this was the greatest feeling I had ever felt.

It changed my life.

I started to believe in myself as a musician. Shortly after that, I started playing the guitar and fell in love with the instrument. I couldn't put it down. The passion for music and now performing started to really burn within me. I decided to move to Los Angeles and attend a prominent music school. I had just gotten married and my wife was a native Californian with family there. It gave her a chance to be close to family and me a chance to pursue a dream. Fortunately, Kameo believed that I could do anything and supported me one hundred percent.

I will never forget the feeling of walking into that school and seeing the tremendous diversity of people in many ways chasing the same dream as me. Sitting next to me was a long-haired "rocker" dressed in all black leather, a Japanese jazz guitarist who couldn't speak English, and a southern rock fan from Texas; and then there was me, a clean-cut kid from Utah.

It soon became clear that it didn't matter where each of us were from; we all had a bond in music and we quickly became friends. I chose to study guitar performance, which was certainly not my best instrument, and I was without a doubt the worst guitarist in the class. After all, I had only been playing a couple years. I remember vividly the first time I was expected to perform a solo in front of the class. Again, total fear hit me, and as I sat down and rested the guitar on my knee, my knee was shaking so badly I couldn't play the guitar. It was jumping around too much. That day the performance failed, and it was very difficult for me. However, as time passed and I performed many, many more times, I got to be fairly comfortable playing in front of people. I worked very hard and my guitar playing really improved. When I graduated I wasn't the best in the class, but I also wasn't the worst. My final project was a short concert in front of several hundred people. I put together a band with some tremendous talent, played some original music, and had the time of my life. I had conquered one of my greatest fears and engulfed myself in my greatest passion. I was truly happy.

I was ready to tackle the music business. Living in Los Angeles is not easy. It is very expensive and requires a lot of sacrifice. I wasn't making much money playing music, so my wife was supporting us. She was the reason I was able to do this, and I am still so grateful for her support. Kameo got pregnant while I was in school, and not too long after I graduated, we were blessed with our first daughter, Alexandria. Unfortunately, the pregnancy and birth was very hard on Kameo and her lupus became very active. She could no longer work, and though I tried I simply was not able to support the family and play music. I decided that I would quit trying to get in the music business and follow my other passion, that of being a strong family man. Something I never regretted.

To some, my dream of being a rock star may appear as a failure but not to me. The few years I spent engaged in that passion are truly among my most treasured memories. Regrets rarely come from the things you have done. No, regrets are almost always the result of things you wish you would have done.

Don't live a life wondering. Live a life doing.

People often say to me that they don't really feel passionate about anything. This can happen when people become depressed and feel lost in the direction of their life. Passions when not used can disappear, but in reality they are dormant waiting for you to revive them. If this is where you are at, try this exercise:

**Reviving Your Passions Exercise**

Things that you are passionate about come from the values you hold dear. In our society today, there is attached to the word "values" a morality that suggests a right and a wrong list of characteristics we all should adopt. That is not what I am talking about. For our purposes "values" are simply the things that are most meaningful to you. What do you value most? Below is a list of values. I would like you to peruse this list and write down the words that are most important to you. Keep in mind this is not a comprehensive list and you can feel free to add your own words to the list. The words you choose should feel like they practically jump out from the other words. Do this quickly without too much thought.

| | |
|---|---|
| Abundance | Affection |
| Acceptance | Aggressiveness |
| Accomplishment | Altruism |
| Achievement | Ambition |
| Acknowledgment | Approval |
| Adoration | Assertiveness |
| Advancement | Assurance |
| Adventure | Attractiveness |
| Balance | Cheerfulness |
| Beauty | Cleanliness |
| Being the best | Comfort |
| Bliss | Commitment |
| Boldness | Community |
| Bravery | Compassion |
| Brilliance | Competence |
| Charity | Competition |

# The Power of Passion

Confidence

Conservation

Conviction

Country

Courage

Courtesy

Creativity

Determination

Devotion

Education

Empathy

Encouragement

Endurance

Energy

Enjoyment

Enthusiasm

Environmentalism

Excellence

Faith

Family

Fidelity

Fitness

Friendliness

Friendship

Fun

Generosity

Gratitude

Harmony

Honesty Sacrifice

Security

Self-control

Selflessness

Self-respect

Sensitivity

Sensuality

Serenity

Service

Spirituality

Spontaneity

Stability

Sympathy

Teaching

Teamwork

Thrift

Traditionalism

Trust

Unity

Virtue

Wisdom

Nature

Patience

Peace

Perfection

Perseverance

Philanthropy

Recreation

Relaxation

Religiousness

Sacredness

Leadership

Love

Loyalty

Marriage

Motivation

Integrity

Intelligence

Intimacy

Inspiration

Humor

Humility

Honor

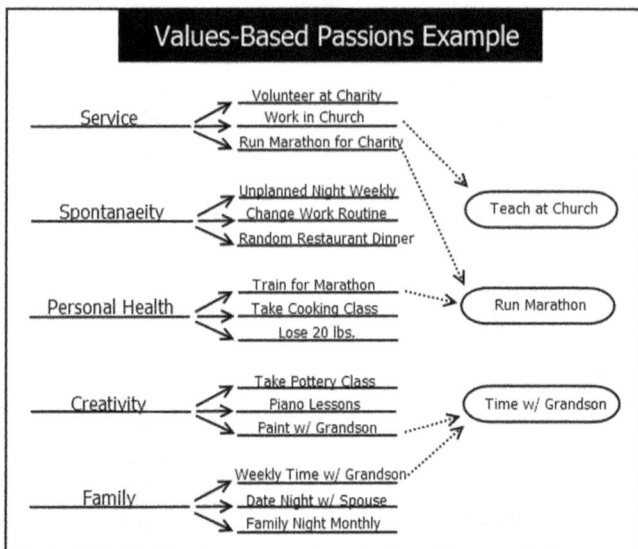

## Values-Based Passions Example

Service
- Volunteer at Charity
- Work in Church
- Run Marathon for Charity

Spontanaeity
- Unplanned Night Weekly
- Change Work Routine
- Random Restaurant Dinner

Personal Health
- Train for Marathon
- Take Cooking Class
- Lose 20 lbs.

Creativity
- Take Pottery Class
- Piano Lessons
- Paint w/ Grandson

Family
- Weekly Time w/ Grandson
- Date Night w/ Spouse
- Family Night Monthly

Teach at Church
Run Marathon
Time w/ Grandson

After you have pared this list down to your chosen values, I would like you to list three ways to express each value. These can be any activity that expresses the value, whether you do it or not. For example, if one of your values is Creativity, three ways you can express creativity are writing, painting, and playing guitar. You may not know how to paint or play the guitar; at this point it doesn't matter if you know how to do the activity.

Let's try one that is a little more difficult. I value Spontaneity. What are three ways of expressing it? How about the next time you go out to dinner you don't pick a restaurant, you just drive and randomly find a restaurant. How about instead of planning each activity on your next vacation, you just decide what to do when you are there. These are simple activities that express the value.

Do this with at least five values. This will give you a list of at least fifteen activities that are unique to your values. There may be things on the list that don't interest you. For example, you may have listed "playing guitar" on your list but really you aren't that interested in the guitar (is that possible?). Simply remove it and put something there that most interests you. In the end you should have things that interest you on the list. Some are activities that you are already very competent in doing, others you may have a desire to learn .

This is a list that will add meaning to your life because it is based on things that are important to you. It is a great way to peel away the distractions in life that get in the way of doing things that enrich your life. Pick something off the list and incorporate it into your life. You may find that it develops into a passion.

Passions are our greatest weapons against unhappiness, especially during times of adversity. If you make a commitment to engage in your passion even for just a few minutes a day, it will change your life. Remember, your mix of passions is unique to you. Only you can know what or how to pursue them. They are a gift to you from God, given out of love to help you find joy in this life. Develop them and you will find an unquenchable happiness; neglect them and they will disappear.

Chapter 6

# The Battle of the Ego

Winners need not win.

Ego has tremendous irony that needs to be investigated, at least on a cursory level, in our pursuit of happiness. In portions of our society, ego is revered and competitions developed to escalate a person's status, almost always at the expense of another person's self-worth. In other social circumstances, ego is looked upon as a character flaw, i.e. religions, charities, etc. Regardless of your current perception of what ego is and does, I assure you the presence of it will affect your happiness and merits our discussion.

Even the most outwardly humble people will recognize themselves in some of this discussion on ego. Ego is far more than conceit or arrogance. Most believe that ego is that level of confidence that goes beyond a healthy self-opinion. However, ego is involved in even the smallest of decisions in our life. I think most of us believe that we have our ego in check and that it has little effect on our lives. The reality is that ego is a predominant element in all of our lives and can truly dictate how we act and the decisions we make. All the while, we often have no idea ego is a significant part of our decision-making process. It is my hope in this chapter that you will start to see how ego is part of your own life and become sensitive to it. It is becoming aware of our own ego that will help us to eliminate its influence on us. As Eckhart Tolle, the author of *A New Earth* suggests, awareness is the antidote to ego.

The first element of ego is our compulsion to enhance our identity through our association with things. Simply, we begin to attach our value to what we have. This starts at a very young age. I remember two of my daughters playing with their toys; one was three years old, the other was just over one. As the younger of the two, Jackie crawled over and took and started playing with Allie's ball, which Allie was no longer using. You would have thought the world had ended for Allie. She started yelling and pushing Jackie, all the while screaming, "That's mine!" She had become tied up in the thinking that the ball was hers. She owned it.

As we grow, the ball becomes cars, houses, boats, country club memberships, and the list continues. Those things become a representation of our own value. If we are driving a Mercedes, then we are successful. If we are a member of the country club, then we are among the elite.

For about twelve years I was in the advertising

business. That business is built on creating added value to a product so when people purchase it, they feel good about themselves and how they are seen by others. Things as simple as what beer you drink are represented as making you appear more masculine and attractive to women. Really? A beer can do all that? Think about some of the "things" you own personally. Tiffany jewelry, Nordstrom apparel, a Jaguar, and the list goes on. In advertising it is called branding, and a company's brand can literally be the most valuable asset it has. Why? Because it causes people to purchase things at prices they would not normally spend, and it makes them feel better about themselves by doing so.

One evening I was having dinner with a client who was a senior marketing vice president of a company that manufactured cheese. The company's cheese was in all of the major grocery store chains and was a fairly significant company in the industry. He explained to me that not only did they make the cheese that was under their own brand, but they in fact made much of the cheese that was labeled under other companies' brands. Literally they made the cheese for their competition, and it was exactly the same as they retailed. He further went on to tell me how the other companies would position the cheese through their own marketing and branding. Some would represent it as the gourmet cheese for those with a discriminating palette. Others would brand it as the value brand for those on a budget. These cheeses sat next to each other on the grocery store shelves. It was all the same cheese, made with exactly the same ingredients, in the same factories. The only difference was the pricing, and that pricing was dictated by what the company told the customer its value was, and the customer accepted it.

Our attachment to things is always connected to ego. The problem is not just that this obsession with things is ego-identifying but that it creates our consumer-based society where the measure of one's progress is always more. The house is no longer big enough, the car is no longer luxurious enough, and the clothes are no longer nice enough. We continue to buy more and more.

Ultimately, things will never bring you happiness, though the chase can go on for a lifetime, if you allow it. At some point you must realize that things are simply a red herring placed there to enrich the ego. The only happiness things bring is that momentary rush that satisfies the ego. After that, the things quickly become just part of life, and true happiness remains elusive. Don't allow yourself to get caught in that belief and seek happiness in things; it will distract you from how to truly become happy.

I would like to expand your definition of what ego is and how it plays in our lives continuously throughout our days. This may seem a little trite, but it is meant to show you how the smallest of things are ego based and derail our happiness. One of my most frustrating times is when I am in a hurry and driving somewhere. Suddenly it seems like everyone on the road has become incapable of driving with any skill. The cars are going slower, drivers don't use their blinkers, and I get cut off excessively. The simple task of driving can suddenly take on an ego-based meaning. People cut me off so I get angry because they came in "my" lane. They are driving too slowly and it is wasting "my" valuable time. We criticize the other drivers and it makes us feel bigger, better than them. At any time during this process, do you think I am feeling happy? Of course not. I am frustrated and increasingly angry. Even with the smallest of things like driving, the presence of ego will not coexist with happiness. The reality is that these people are doing what they think is best for them and have no interest in injuring me. But for some reason, even the most mundane of activities like driving can involve the negativity of ego.

Complaining nurtures the ego. I bet you have never looked at it that way. Let me explain. Every time we complain about something we are building our ego. When we complain, we are telling a story that shows how something or someone didn't treat us the way we should be treated. The worst form of complaining is when it is directed at another person. This complaining can be to ourselves or to others in the form of gossiping. The next time you are huddled in a group of people and gossiping starts up, notice how the people doing the talking are using their words. You will hear things such as "I wouldn't do that" or perhaps "She is wrong." As you listen you will notice that the words are about elevating the person talking. By demeaning another person, people are essentially trying to feel better about themselves. That is ego.

This is not to suggest that you should not inform someone of a mistake or a deficiency in order to get something right. It also certainly doesn't mean you should tolerate poor behavior. There is no ego involved if you send your steak back because it is too rare. However, it is important to stick to the facts. The ego becomes involved when you take offense to or act personally attacked by another. If you sent your steak back and made it about someone else being wrong, then ego becomes involved. For example, if you told your waiter, "I specifically asked for this steak to be well done, but you or your cook can't seem to get it right." The goal at that point isn't to get the steak correct; it is to make the cook and the waiter feel inadequate. Compare that to "Excuse me, my steak is a little rare; would you mind cooking it to well done?" You will notice some people will take advantage of every injustice done to them as an opportunity to enhance their ego. You see it in boardrooms when high-powered executives belittle their subordinates. You see it in grocery stores when a person berates a cashier for having had to wait in line too long. Choose your words carefully and make certain that the objective is to get "the steak right," not make someone feel badly and yourself superior.

Earlier I stated that awareness is the antidote to ego. Simply, by listening and being aware of the voice in your head as it begins to complain or demean another will stop the process that feeds ego. Again, ego and awareness cannot coexist.

I have a dear friend who has been married to his wife for nearly thirty years. One day as we were talking, I asked him how he was able to do that. How can a relationship be nurtured, developed, and stronger today than it was thirty years ago? His comment to me was "Mylie is always right." He had a huge smile on his face when he said this. Is Mylie always right? I very much doubt that. But what my friend was saying is that his relationship didn't require him to win the arguments. There doesn't need to be someone who is right or wrong. By taking that position, peace prevailed, and though disagreements occurred they didn't become hurtful because ego was not a part of the relationship. He didn't need to win. This philosophy works in all relationships, even difficult or adversarial relationships.

Being right is one of the most damaging things that grow the negativity of an ego. Does that make sense to you? If you are right, shouldn't that give you a pass for having an ego? Remember, when you are right and recognize your superiority, you are feeding your ego. Having done something correctly no longer is what is important, rather the emphasis shifts to being superior to others. Being correct is never a justification for pointing out that someone else is wrong. The first line in this chapter says, "Winners need not win." It does not imply that winners don't win, nor does it suggest winners choose not to win. Simply, it says winners *need* not win because their egos need not be fed.

So why in the world would I include a chapter on ego in a book about finding joy during times of adversity? Since ego causes people to view themselves as better than another person, even for just a moment, it undercuts the process of loving others. In ego there is conflict and negativity, a winner and a loser. In love there can be none of those traits.

# Chapter 7

## A Word on Guilt

Useless.

# Chapter 8

# Peace*maker* Not Peace*finder*

The Dalai Lama was recently speaking in San Diego, California. He told a story of a monk with whom he had spoken. This monk had been imprisoned as a political prisoner in China for forty years. Imagine the life lost and the horrendous injustice to this man. The loss of relationships with family and friends was tragic, not to mention the constant loneliness he must have felt. For what? Being a peaceful protestor against tyranny. When his friend was released, the Dalai Lama asked him what his greatest fear was during his imprisonment. You would expect to hear stories of torture and isolation, but that is not what was said. "That I may lose compassion for my captors" was his response.

Imagine that, the denial of a life with all of its many experiences for a life in a box, and his greatest fear was that he may lose compassion for his captors.

While most of us won't be required to generate an inner peace in such circumstances, we all will need to choose peace over conflict and ego virtually every day of our lives. Some people look at a person's choice to not "defend himself" as weakness. In reality choosing one's battles very carefully and opting for peace takes enormous strength. We all innately feel we are correct in our opinions and often feel personally attacked if our view is not shared by others. We must realize that our opinions are simply perceptions that we have, just as another person's opinions are only his or her perceptions. You may ultimately be right, but most often the battle to prove it doesn't justify the expense that conflict brings. Inner peace requires confidence and maturity and with that comes the knowledge that conflict in any form cannot coexist with peace, love, and kindness; and it is in peace, love, and kindness that we find joy.

Do you want happiness? Then you must make peace.

In the Sermon on the Mount in the New Testament, Jesus lists some traits that he wanted his people to understand. In one of those statements he teaches, "Blessed be the peacemakers, for they shall be the children of God." He then went on to live a life based on peace, despite the denigrations and humiliations he suffered. He knew he was correct in his statements, but rather than argue his points of view, he chose peace rather than conflict. Conflict he knew he could win. Christians and non-Christians alike can appreciate the principles taught by this humble life.

Notice the word often used with a person of peace is peace*maker*. It is not peace*finder* or peace*hope-it-comes-along*, it is peacemaker. One who *makes* peace. When you make something, virtually anything, it requires effort and some level of commitment. Peace is no different. It is not found in passivity; one must show strength and commitment to it. While peace is generally easy to allow during times without dissension, it is those moments where differences of opinion arise that truly show one's commitment to peace. Any relenting to conflict will cause peace to diminish and the conflict to escalate.

I think many people will find that at times the most challenging place in which to find peace and harmony is in the walls of their own home. We don't have the pressures of cultural politeness to force our behavior with our family. Additionally, we have an expected hierarchy in a family that can dictate the relative importance of each member of the family's opinion. For example, in families parents are typically the leaders over the children, and obedience is expected but oftentimes not given (teenagers?). As a child grows and begins to exert his or her own autonomy, the authoritative parent may suppress the child's behavior rather than guide it to more appropriate expressions, leading to conflict and rebellion. Obviously children acquire wisdom as they gain experience, and naturally this leads to different points of view. The conflict in a family occurs when opinions collide and there is little acceptance of the other's viewpoint, regardless of the position in the family hierarchy. The wise parent avoids conflict and maintains peace by managing his or her children's behavior and respecting their opinion, rather that dictating it. This is choosing peace and ignoring that pesky ego we all have.

Some of the most valuable books I have read that have helped me understand and choose peace are not books on peace at all. I have found that "how-to" books on parenting are invaluable in teaching us how to be peaceful in times of conflict. As we have discussed, conflict can quickly escalate and peace dissipate in any relationship unless someone chooses peace and responds appropriately to make it happen. The same skills used in good parenting are almost always applicable to our other relationships as well. Strong, capable parents do not respond to their children's emotional and occasionally cruel outbursts. They maintain peace by controlling their emotions, and rather than being defensive, they exhibit increased love and logic. This in no way means they accept poor behavior or disrespect, they just respond in such a way that doesn't escalate contention. It is really hard for a fight to escalate when one of the participants is continually reaffirming their love for the other and commitment to their well-being.

I have been fishing on the ocean once...and only once. My brother and I boarded a boat with about forty other people in Oxnard, California, an hour or so outside of Los Angeles. We were excited because neither of us had fished for red snapper before and thought it would be an adventure. We were right; it was an adventure but not the one we were looking for.

Red snapper are fairly small fish and are found about a thousand feet deep in the ocean. You fish for them using a very stiff rod with several different leaders with hooks on them, and a very heavy weight on the end to drag the line down the length of a few football fields. Imagine a line with a full can of soda pop on the end. That is what if felt like.

I had grown up fishing in the lakes and rivers of Wyoming and Utah. I knew a fair amount about fishing for trout; you would cast the line out and wait for the fish to come to dinner. Not so with red snapper. All you would do is drop the weight over the side of the boat and let it sink and sink and sink. Then after some time the boat captain would yell, "Reel them in and let's see if anyone caught one." The line was so deep that if you had a fish on the line, you didn't know it. There was no tugging or movement of any kind. We would then spend the next half hour reeling in the line to see if we had a fish. Further, if you had a fish on your line, it would be dead when it surfaced because bringing it up from that depth so quickly would cause pressure problems and kill the fish well before it got to the boat. You may be getting the picture that this could be the most boring fishing one could ever participate in. It took you forty-five minutes to do an exhausting round trip with your hooks, and you didn't know you had anything until that laborious routine was completed.

It gets worse.

On this particular day, the captain's fish finder was not seeing anything. After two hours of fishing not a single soul had caught a fish. The boat staff was getting a little panicked because we all paid a significant amount of money to be there and catch some ocean delicacies. The captain announced that they were having trouble, and he was going to take us an hour in a different direction to see if we could find the elusive snappers elsewhere. When we finally arrived at the new destination, the captain could see a school of fish with his fish finder and he told us to drop our lines. Finally, after nearly a half-day of "fishing," about five other people and I dragged up a snapper with its eyes popped out an inch because of the change of pressure. At this point even the boredom of landing one of these ocean dwellers was better than nothing at all, and the excitement on the boat set in. The captain again announced enthusiastically, "OK, drop those lines back in and let's catch some more." As I dropped the line over the side of the boat, one of the large ocean hooks lodged itself deeply into my index finger. That heavy weight on the end dropped ten feet and never reached the water. It was as if a miniature bungee jumper leaped off the boat and then bounced back and forth, each time embedding the hook deeper into my finger.

Just at the moment when we were smelling success, I got injured. The captain came to look at my finger, and I could tell the pressure he was feeling earlier because of the lack of fish had increased tenfold. He suggested we just take the needle-nose pliers and tear the hook out. Anyone with an ounce of sense knew that this would have gutted most of my finger. I was a guitarist in music school at the time and risking a finger was not an option. Hesitantly, the captain returned to his chair, lifted the PA, and announced to everyone that there was an injury and the rest of the trip would need to be canceled. I was now the least popular person in Southern California, and there was talk of throwing me overboard. Two hours later we arrived back at the dock, and I went to the emergency room and had the hook pushed through my finger. To this day, part of my finger is numb.

This was relatively a minor injury yet it became the focus of everyone on board. For me it was quite painful and I couldn't think of much else. To everyone around me it at least ruined their fishing experience. However, I maintain I did them all a favor getting them away from that horrendously boring fishing excursion. Regardless, everyone's focus was on that single event, and my focus was exclusively on my injury. No one was focused on what they came for: fishing.

Conflict is much like my fishing injury. It deters everyone's focus on the things that are most important and causes them to focus on the conflict. Have you ever gotten into an argument that became very heated and couldn't remember the reason it started? As we strive to become peacemakers, we must recognize the seedlings of conflict and stop them from growing. While this is very difficult, conflict and dissension are far more painful and ultimately damaging to everyone's life. By the way, if I had my choice to do it over again, I would have just pushed the hook through my finger on the boat. Though it sounds incredibly painful, that would have solved the problem for everyone and got all of us back to fishing for a twelve-inch, prize trophy red snapper.

A discussion on peace would be incomplete without including the principle of forgiveness. Much is said on this topic, and there are a variety of opinions on the matter. In the context of this book where we are trying to allow our lives to be filled with happiness, forgiveness is critical and entirely for the forgiver's benefit. In other words, forgiving someone is for you, not them. You will often see someone who is a victim of crime interviewed and say, "I can forgive, but I can't forget." Unfortunately, they then carry the painful burden of hatred throughout their lives. That hatred can ruin the joy that they could have in their life because they can't truly forgive.

We do not judge anyone who refuses to forgive. We have not walked in his or her shoes. But when assessing our own lives, we must face our demons and see what grudges we are carrying. There is an inevitable truth that says any grudge against another, even if justified, diminishes or even eliminates a person's happiness.

I was meeting one day with Jan, my Life Coach and counselor. She has been a remarkable influence for good in my life. Someone very close to me had done something unbelievably cruel and I was hurt tremendously. I was explaining the situation to Jan, and she listened intently, allowing me to spew my thoughts of anger and betrayal. At the end I paused and waited for her response, expecting support and justification for my feelings, but she replied, "Jack, your friend isn't hurting over this, she is enjoying her life. Why are you carrying the pain and not enjoying your life because of something *she* did?" It became clear to me at that moment, forgiveness allows for the happiness of the forgiver and is completely independent of the forgiven.

To truly be a person of peace takes skill in most of the areas mentioned in this book. People must have confidence in themselves, love unconditionally, be able to control their thoughts and actions, eliminate ego, and forgive. No wonder Jesus said, "Blessed is the peacemaker." For one who truly possesses such attributes is an amazing person. While this may feel daunting to most of us who recognize our weaknesses, every step we make toward becoming a peacemaker will increase the overall joy and happiness in our life. If for no other reason than because we will have reduced the contention in our life; and when contention is absent peace, love, and kindness abound.

# Chapter 9

# The Parasite of Fear

What is a parasite? It is something that lives solely on another. Vampire bats suck the blood from cattle. Some parasites may live in a person's intestinal track. Big, ugly, long tape worms. Parasites conjure up a vision that most of us find disgusting. The parasite of fear should conjure up that same feeling of disgust.

Fear, not hate, is the opposite of love. It is from fear that other negative emotions spawn. Feelings of hate, jealousy, and selfishness all can be traced to an origin of fear. If love brings us happiness, it would stand to reason that fear is the ultimate risk to that happiness. We can be doing everything right–developing love for ourselves and others, identifying the passions that move our spirit, eliminating negativity from our life–but unless we learn to manage our fear, we may never attain true happiness. The attraction to the negative will begin to creep back in.

Everyone feels fear; it is OK to feel fear. We are designed to protect ourselves from harm; fear is our "call to arms." There are two responses to fear: 1) It heightens our abilities; 2) It paralyzes us. Now, given that we know we will feel fear, we must learn to manage it and direct it to heighten our abilities. However, if we choose the response that allows fear to paralyze us, it can stop us from following our dreams. Fear can reinforce negative self-talk. Fear can make us hate. Fear can undo all the positive work in your life.

Fear is a magnifying glass in our life. Think about this: when you use a magnifying glass, you are not enlarging what you are looking at; you are simply altering your perception of what it is you are viewing. Fear does the same thing in our world. It causes you to focus on that thing that you are afraid of, and as you focus on the problem or element of your fear, it gets bigger and bigger until you are ignoring all the other positive, wonderful elements in your life. Then fear controls you, and you assume the worst *and* experience failure because you were too afraid to move forward. Now not only have you not been enjoying the wonderful things in your life because you are focusing on your fear, but also you fail because fear magnifies and paralyzes you. Ultimately, fear, and the failure it brings, is unpleasant and so you start avoiding anything with risk in your life. You settle for an average job, relationship, home, etc., but at least you don't feel afraid. Is that really a trade you are willing to make?

Have you ever been afraid to approach

someone, maybe an attractive person of the opposite sex? As we ponder how we will walk up to this person, what we will say, and how we will say it, we start to assume this person will respond to us negatively. Fear causes us to look at the worst-case scenario–she'll reject me, she is too pretty for me, she hasn't even noticed me, etc.–all before you have even said a word to her. But have you ever talked to someone you were afraid of talking to and then said afterward, "That wasn't so bad"? Here's another simple example. Have you ever been fearful of an amusement park ride, participated in it anyway, and then, after you finished, you not only said, "That wasn't so bad," but also said, "That was awesome!"

Fear keeps us from enjoying the "awesome."

Adam Honnald may be the mentally strongest person I have witnessed. Normally he is known for his physical strength. Adam is a twenty-six-year-old mountain climber and has climbed some of the most harrowing mountains on the planet...without ropes, without help. Imagine climbing a rock face of a mountain straight up for sixteen hundred feet. He often is hanging with all of his weight being held by only his fingertips. Any slip, even the smallest of mistakes, would result in certain death. That is a very physically strong person.

But think for a moment about the strength he has mentally. When you free-form climb, it is nearly impossible to stop climbing and go back down. Simply, going down to safety is harder than going up and is not an option. What can happen to climbers is that they reach a place on the face of the mountain that feels impossible to climb. Their arms and feet may be too tired, or they just can't find the cracks to jam their fingers into to give them the leverage to climb. This is where the strength of the mind must kick in. Fear starts to creep in and very quickly the climber can be overcome and frozen to the face of the cliff. They can neither go up nor down, and that sense of panic completely paralyzes them. For many who have experienced this, it has brought the ultimately penalty. Death.

When Alex climbs he seems to simply ignore any fear. That does not mean it isn't there waiting to pounce on him. It means he uses his mind to manage fear, even whistling as he climbs the most difficult phases. Now he is in top physical condition and seems to know his limitations...if there are any. Certainly being aware of one's capabilities fuels confidence and provides a barrier against fear. That must be nurtured in whatever we want to accomplish. If we want to start a new relationship, we need to be that which we want to attract. If we want a kind, confident, independent partner, we need to be kind, confident, and independent. If we want someone who is physically fit and lives a healthy lifestyle, we need to be physically fit and live a healthy lifestyle.

So often someone will yearn for a relationship. They feel lonely, sad, and unhappy. They think, "If only I had someone in my life, I wouldn't be lonely and would be so happy." Unfortunately, feeling lonely, sad, and unhappy attracts sadness, loneliness, and ultimately unhappiness. Even if a person attracts someone while feeling these negative emotions, the person attracted will only reinforce these feelings. Believe me, you can feel incredible loneliness in a room full of people. And the worst loneliness may be when you are with your partner and have nothing between you.

Get yourself in that same place as that you want to attract. It isn't easy, but it is necessary. Once you have gotten there, you will have confidence that you haven't previously felt. You will then be ready when doubt rears its ugliness and fear comes to derail you. As Adam Honnald does, you simply whistle and ignore it, and go forward. By doing that, fear heightens your skills and drives you further than you may have gone without it. It stays a positive thing, and fear was meant to be positive.

Imagine the feeling Adam must get when he meets his challenge. Imagine doing something nobody thought you could do. That is living life as it should be.

Fear has a left jab called doubt. Just like a boxer leads with a jab over and over, it is never the jab that knocks you out. It's that big punch waiting in the wings. As you start to get beat down by the jab of doubt, the knockout punch of fear is in the wings. Stay protected, and neither can get you. Let your guard down, and it's lights out. Manage your fear and you are on your way to a thrilling, passion-filled life.

**Top Five Excuses Fear Generates**

Fear generally starts with excuses. Excuses that slowly build until there are enough reasons to justify not moving forward with something you desire. The subtlety of fear is the snare. Be on the lookout for these excuses. They are simply disguises fear uses to ensure that you live a life of mediocrity.

## 1.    It is too hard.

Achieving a life that is filled with joy despite the adversity you may be experiencing may feel difficult. But remember you are exchanging sadness, pain, and unhappiness for this hard work. Ultimately, living with that pain is actually the hard work. Making the change to incorporating your passions into your life will be easy. Let your mind accept this truth. It will be easy because you are meant to be happy. Joy is what God wants you to have. It is important to recognize this excuse as a falsehood meant to convince you to settle.

## 2.    There is too much risk.

You have a destiny. Think about that, you have a destiny to fulfill. Now certainly there are times that responsibility and duty block your ability to take risk. For me it was so hard to leave the business world to follow my passions. I had a family to support. I had a respectable job. My duties kept me from following my God-given plan. Finally, it became apparent that my personal well-being was at stake. If taking risk is simply overwhelming, you need to slowly incorporate your passions. You will see that the excuse of too much risk is a red herring. Risk is real and failure is a possibility. But you must understand that failure is simply a flat tire on your trip of life. If you are driving on a long-distance trip and you get a flat tire, do you just stop there and not continue with the trip? Of course not. You fix the flat and continue on with the trip. Risk is scary, but you will never truly be happy until you fully commit to your convictions and destiny. The reality is that not taking risk is the riskiest thing of all.

**3.    It will take too long.**

We are often told we need to have patience in this life. Patience has never been my greatest strength, and so time has been one of my own most difficult excuses to overcome. One thing that helps me is to not use the word "patience," but rather use the word "allow." There is some negativity associated with the word "patience." It suggests time is a struggle that one must endure. Rather we need to look at time as a series of moments that allow your destiny to be fulfilled. The universe is furiously working to ensure you are attracting happiness. You simply need to allow it to occur. Of course it may take you time to develop skills, return to school, or engage in another activity to build your talents. But keep in mind, time moves forward whether you are pursuing happiness or reinforcing mediocrity. In four years from now you will be four years older, whether you choose to pursue something that will bring you happiness or not. You might as well choose happiness.

## 4.  I'm too busy.

The things that make your life too busy are rarely the things that matter most. Obviously caring for family and employment are critical, but if you are truly honest with yourself, you will find a host of things that suck your time and are not nearly as important as pursuing your passions. Organize and declutter your life and you can find time. It may take sacrifice, but you will be sacrificing those things that are not as important for those things that develop long-lasting happiness.

## 5.  I can't afford it.

Remember the Cornerstone Statement I introduced earlier? In it I say "I am worthy of unlimited abundance and prosperity." You must feel this to your core. You are worthy of anything that helps you realize your dreams, and this often requires money. The excuse of not having money only reinforces images that are not in harmony with the vision of the Cornerstone Statement. The universe has plenty of resources for all of us to reach our dreams. There *is* unlimited abundance. You will attract it.

Recently I was watching a movie called *We*

## The Parasite of Fear

*Bought a Zoo*, starring Matt Damon and based on Benjamin Mee's memoir. It is a fun family film with an engaging story, especially for animal lovers, of which I am one. But there was one thing in the story that struck me as profound. In the story Matt Damon's character is taught a lesson by his brother. He is told that if he will commit to showing twenty seconds of absolute courage in facing his fears, it will change his life. Simply, only commit to yourself that you will be flawlessly courageous for twenty seconds when you are afraid. If you do so, you will overcome some of your greatest challenges. In the story he used that "rule" to have the courage to ask a beautiful young woman out, and she later became his wife. Had he not shown twenty seconds of courage, he would have never met his wife.

Almost all of our fears subside after we take the initial step. Whether it is a phone call that we are afraid to make, a paper we are afraid to sign, or a love we are afraid to share; by showing twenty seconds of absolute courage, we will learn to manage and overcome our fear. A great place to start in managing our fear is to implement the twenty-second rule.

Fear is indeed a parasite. Unfortunately, we sometimes don't realize what it is doing to derail our happiness because it is so subtle. Fear is the opposite of love for that reason. Watch it closely. When you see excuses for not pursuing something meaningful to you, it is the beginning of fear and the magnifying of negativity. Catch fear in its beginning stages and do not focus on it or allow it to take hold. Manage your fear and make it a source of heightening your abilities, rather than paralyzing you from action, and you will have removed the number one stumbling block to happiness.

Chapter 10

# The Role of Adversity

As I write this, there is a popular song by Kelly Clarkson that says, "What doesn't kill you makes you stronger." We have all heard this many times in our life. I have often joked that I would happily accept being weak to have avoided the adversity placed in my path. Many people who are reading this are at this moment struggling with intense adversity. They may have been victims of crime, felt tremendous despair at the death of a partner or child, and many other serious challenges. When my wife died, people would often say things like "you will love again," or "she's in a better place." People would tell me, "Life will get better; it may take a few years, but it will get better." A few years! All I knew was that I found every moment of every day to be painful without any relief. Just making it from the morning to the evening felt nearly impossible. I couldn't even comprehend a few years.

But here I am fifteen years later...happy.

I spoke at Kameo's funeral. I really felt that I knew her better than anyone else and a tribute to her without my insight would be incomplete. It was a wonderful funeral. There were many moments shared by those who loved my wife that honored her for the life that she lived. Imagine being at a funeral where the person who had died was only thirty-five years old and had left a husband and three young girls under the age of eight. That feels so sad. That was the situation I was in, and I could feel the heaviness of sadness in the room. My girls, all wearing beautifully matching dresses, and I sat in the front row. I was the final speaker. When I walked up to the podium, I knew that either people would walk away from this funeral feeling inspired, or they would leave feeling awful, encumbered with sadness. I wanted them to feel inspired.

To ease the tension, I started with a fairly inappropriate joke. "My wife was always joking about being flat chested and said to me a couple weeks before she died that she looked forward to being in the hereafter because she was going to get bigger boobs." I then said, "That gives us both a reason to look forward to heaven." The congregation felt a tremendous relief as the moment was met with laughter rather than tears.

I then told a story that will forever be with me. The month before Kameo died we had taken my oldest two daughters, Allie and Jackie, to Arches National Park in Moab, Utah. We had rented an RV and traveled there and planned on doing quite a bit of hiking. It is a stunning place filled with incredible beauty. We hiked through caverns and even crawled through tight spaces to enjoy the park. Kameo had lupus, a chronic disease that can impact almost any part of a body. She had serious arthritis and would often experience lupus flares. This would cause her to get a high fever, her joints would get very painful making it difficult to walk, and she would be exhausted. The only thing she could do was take some meds and sleep for the day. Coming into this vacation we knew that it could be difficult for her, but she had had one of the best years of health since we were married. She felt that she could manage this trip.

On our final day in Arches, we decided to climb to Delicate Arch. This is a fairly long hike and my girls were really young. I was worried that they may not make it. The morning before the hike Kameo started feeling badly. Her joints were starting to hurt, and she started getting a fever. It was a lupus flare. If we were not careful, a lupus flare could get bad enough that we would need to go to the hospital. We decided that Kameo would be OK but needed to just sleep in the RV while I took the girls to Delicate Arch.

After hours of hiking and seeing one of the most beautiful places I had ever seen, we started back down the mountain. We were about a half mile from the finish line when just ahead of us we saw Kameo coming up the mountain. When we reached her, I asked her what she was doing. Her response was simply "I just really needed to be with you guys." Even today, fifteen years later, I see those moments as clearly as I ever have. It wasn't even that eventful of a moment. But the feeling of love I felt just those few weeks before her death would forever be with me. She just really needed to be with us.

During that time of adversity I rested with that wonderful memory.

What is the role of adversity? It isn't to make us stronger, as many people believe. It does make us stronger, but that is not its primary purpose. I believe adversity is given to us to help us be empathetic. It eliminates our ego quickly, and the foundation of ego is selfishness. Adversity allows us to be humble and feel emotions, understand other people, and direct our efforts to others rather than ourselves, if we choose to respond that way. I am convinced that if there were no adversity, our lives would be self-absorbed, and there would be no empathy, no love, and ultimately no happiness. This being the case, adversity brings us happiness.

Sure doesn't feel like it though, does it?

Ram Dass is a great spiritual leader in the West though his teachings are very much Eastern-influenced philosophies. He was closely associated with Timothy Leary and was fired from Harvard in the late sixties. He went on a spiritual quest for many years and truly became a humble servant of mankind and of God. One of my dearest friends and his wife met him for the first time at his home in Hawaii. Ram Dass had a stroke in the nineties that left him incapacitated on one side and wheelchair bound for life. In this meeting my friend asked him how he has done since his stroke. The response was enlightening. Ram Dass hugged himself with his right side overlapping his stagnant left side, while repeating the words, "I love my stroke, I love my stroke."

For many of us this would seem like a disingenuous declaration, but to a man who had committed himself to a spiritual understanding of life, it should be seen as enlightened understanding of adversity. He had embraced his stroke as an adversity that gave him even more of an ability to love others at a greater level than he previously had been able. The humility provided by the stroke gave him an even deeper empathy and understanding of other people. I believe he understands that his stroke brought greater happiness to his life that ultimately he would not have had without it.

This seems difficult to believe for all of us. How could a person be grateful for such adversity? When you breakdown the actual results of adversity, you get a glimpse of how it can impact a life for good. Certainly the immobilization of his body must have been very difficult to accept; certainly the recovery was enormous. But when all is said and done, that became an acceptable trade-off for a greater understanding of mankind, a deeper empathy for others' challenges, and ultimately a closer connection to God. Ram Dass loves his stroke.

Today as I write this, it is a beautiful April spring

day in South Jordan, Utah. The birds are singing, the sky is perfectly blue, and I left a very challenging funeral just a few hours ago. A young man had taken his own life, a man I knew fairly well and whose family is as close to me as my own family. I saw the weeping of a brokenhearted mother, the painful spoken words of friends, and despair by all that was heavy and palpable. But as the meeting progressed, I saw an interesting development. People were joined together in sharing story after story of the goodness of this young man. You could feel the emphasis shift from a self-inflicted death to a life lived that brought joy to many people. There were smiles on people's faces as they remembered long-forgotten memories of their loved one. It was beautiful to see that even in this most tragic of situations, it was bringing members of his family closer together, more dependent on each other, more loving to one another. The foundation to building a stronger, more loving and empathetic family had begun already.

It is important to me that we don't minimize the pain and grief associated with such adversity. Such pain really can't be understood by most of us. It feels completely devastating. With that said, if a person chooses to see such adversity and its role in developing him or her, they will come out of this devastating time a kinder, more loving, and yes, stronger person than before. That person will one day enjoy a deeper understanding of life and feel tremendous joy.

One last thought: I have said several times throughout this book that these thoughts that I have shared are based on my experiences and how following the principles have dramatically changed my life and brought me unbridled happiness, despite significant adversity. I believe the principle that adversity brings happiness is true for everyone, but not everyone is ready to understand this. If this sounds truly unrealistic to you, it is simply not the right time yet. Keep an open mind. Be aware of how adversity affects you and those around you, and apply what you learn. You will be shocked at how this new paradigm can change your world.

Chapter 11

# How to Be Sad Without Being Miserable

Sadness and grieving have a place in life. To not grieve over a significant loss only delays healing and can cause difficulties in other areas of your life. Grief will also help you be more understanding and compassionate with others. Feeling pain is part of life. The year my wife Kameo died several other very important people in my life passed away, including my dear grandfather, biological father, aunt Rosemary, who was my second mother, and a friend. It was a dark year. I remember sitting at my aunt's funeral reading a book on piloting a Cessna 172. I was ignoring the service, but more importantly I was ignoring my pain.

My aunt Rosemary was a huge part of my growing-up years. She went to my recitals, school plays, and any other event I participated in. I would spend hours with her family, and my cousin Renae was one of my closest friends. I adored my aunt. This was the death of one of the most important people in my life, and I was feeling nothing, rather I wasn't allowing myself to feel anything.

It didn't occur to me at the time that I had quit feeling pain; in fact, I had quit feeling anything. Repeated adversity can make you unfeeling and have diminished compassion toward others if you choose to respond to it that way, as did I. It can make you harsh and judgmental of others. Don't make that choice; at some point you will have to revisit the pain and it will be no easier then, than it is to deal with now. Allow yourself to feel your pain, travel through the grief, and come out the other end.

More often than not feeling the pain at all is getting stalled in the grief. Sadness is a part of life. Even Jesus wept with the family of Lazarus who were grieving over his death. To be sad is appropriate. The danger is when we get stuck in pain and it begins to feed on itself and becomes depression. Believe me, when sadness develops into the illness of depression, it can spiral into a darkness that is unimaginable. When depression is active, a person is no more able to "just pull up his or her bootstraps" and get over it, than a diabetic is able to just quit being a diabetic. It requires help from others, especially professionals, and there should be no hesitation to seek that.

However, I have found that when adversity is in my life I can control its impact and not allow it to control me or "stall" me into depression. The first step is understanding the role of adversity. Adversity has a divine purpose and it isn't arbitrary. You are asked to travel through the pain of tragedy for a purpose. It may not be a purpose you want to accept, or the purpose may not be immediately apparent. But all adversity has a divine purpose. Most importantly, if you choose to survive your adversity and not allow it to derail or ruin your life, you will come out of it a stronger, kinder, more compassionate and empathetic person. Those traits are part of the persona of God. Understanding that there is purpose in adversity will help you push through it as you look for the greater meaning behind the pain.

The next step in controlling the impact of adversity is to understand that all adversity is external. The great spiritual leaders throughout history have all taught that peace is found within. No matter what is going on outside of you, your life can be peaceful inside. I encourage you to frequently spend time with yourself in quiet solitude, feeling that peace that comes from within. Nothing can be said, no pain can be exerted, no loss can be felt, that can take away your internal peace. Only you can allow that. Viktor Frankl's classic book *Man's Search for Meaning* details his own battles to understand this principle. Having been imprisoned in a concentration camp, watched friends and family brutally murdered, and forced to live in unimaginable conditions, he spent time learning the external nature of adversity and that his ultimate control was in his internal, peaceful world. It is in that world that you will find understanding from God and the peace we all crave.

How do we do this? When we are in the middle of tragedy, often we are overwhelmed with thoughts of the adversity. Nearly every waking moment can be engulfed by thoughts of the challenges facing you. Sometimes the moments that you are alone can be the most painful as you end up completely thinking of your pain, with nothing to distract you. Surprisingly for me, my peaceful moment is usually done in the presence of many people when I go to the gym. I turn on inspirational music–oftentimes peaceful, gentle music, which is not what most people play during their workouts–and I talk to God in my mind. That is when I find my inner peace, especially during times of adversity. I actually picked some of my favorite inspirational songs and put them on my iPod specifically for my workouts. I have found that I am most effective feeling divinity when I am focusing on my physical, spiritual, and emotional needs simultaneously. I recommend you try it. Some people find this peace kneeling at their bedside in prayer, attending a religious service, hiking in the mountains, or some other process. Whatever it is that helps you connect with divinity, do it daily, especially during times of adversity.

There cannot be enough said about the power of gratitude in helping you to control the despair that can come from adversity. Certainly start every day thanking God for the blessings in your life. There was a time when I literally had lost every material thing in my life. I went from an eight-bedroom home with a fair amount of personal comfort to a very small apartment. Every item of any value that I owned had been sold or taken away. It was interesting to me that after all this loss, the list of what I was grateful for hadn't changed. My beautiful daughters, my friends, my parents, my health, and even my dogs were what meant so much to me. My gratitude was and continues to be full.

Gratitude helps you focus on that which is truly meaningful. Even when you are suffering with the most difficult of challenges, you can find things for which you are grateful. Remind yourself of those things routinely and you will mitigate the impact of adversity.

Remember our goal is to accept the sadness that adversity can bring without it derailing or ruining our lives. We all know or have heard of someone who has had a terrible event ruin his or her life. Many times the tragedy is so intense that the destruction of the person's life seems inevitable. Events like the death of a spouse or child, being a victim of a heinous crime, or serious loss of health can easily ruin a life if a person lets it. It is understandable. But being understandable doesn't mean it needs to be acceptable. Rather than turn to alcohol or drugs or some other artificial self-medication, a person can turn to the principles in this book, grieve *and* survive, becoming a stronger and better person. I say this in no way meaning to diminish the severity of a person's adversity. Some adversity seems incomprehensible, but I assure you I know from where I speak. Greet tragedy with the principles I am discussing and you will survive and survive well.

Find comfort in the love of others, but be aware their efforts to comfort with words will not necessarily help, and may frustrate you. Just feel their love, accept it with gratitude, and let that fill your emotional bank account. A few hours after my wife's funeral I was sitting in my living room with a friend; I am sure the silence in that room must have been very difficult for him. What do you say to someone who had just attended his wife's funeral? Searching for words to comfort me, he said, "When things settle down, I have a single neighbor that I would like you to meet." Yes, he wanted to line me up the day of my wife's funeral.

People who are closest to us want to fix our problems. In my case, this friend saw that I was hurting because of the death of my wife. Foolishly in the moment he tried to fix it by getting me a new wife. Not everyone is so misguided as was my friend, and I doubt he would have said that had he not been in such unfamiliar territory emotionally speaking, but there will be times people reach out to you. Let them comfort you, let them be there for you; and when they try and help you with advice that may be off track, simply smile and accept it for what it is: an expression of love. Don't allow it to add to your pain.

Really the best thing most people can do when a friend is struggling is be available to listen. Certainly if a person has gone through a similar experience, then advice may be valuable. But most people going through adversity need the support of a listening ear much more than a talking mouth.

Nothing can be better for the soul than serving others. It truly can be the cure to the pain caused by adversity. I have a friend who is a burn victim, and she found great healing helping other burn victims by volunteering at the burn center. She did this while she herself was healing. One day she arrived at the burn center and this beautiful child was screaming and out of control. She was covered in burn scarring, having suffered tremendous tragedy. Her mother's boyfriend had tried to murder them by burning their house down. This sweet girl hadn't been able to get out of the house but somehow survived.

With burn victims the emotional impact can be as great as the physical destruction. The disfigurement can lead to stares and insensitive comments by others. The burn center was having a pool party, and this girl didn't want to have others see her scars. She felt ugly and embarrassed and was lashing out at those around her. My friend was able to take this young girl into a quiet room, calm her down, and talk to her. She started by showing this girl her own scars and telling of the pain she had endured. Quickly there was a bond that only someone who had suffered a similar tragedy could establish. Before too long my friend and the young girl were both in the pool playing together. Both my friend and this girl felt healing that day. Service indeed can be an elixir for personal adversity.

Being sad is not a sign of weakness. Some people try to be strong during times of adversity by ignoring it. Others get so intertwined with their adversity that it becomes who they are, and they never seem to be able to get through it. Feel the pain and sadness that adversity has placed before you, but choose to move through it. There may be moments when that feels completely impossible. Those moments will fade but will require some strength on your part. You will need to understand the role of adversity by searching for your internal place of peace, find gratitude in the many other areas of your life, and provide service to others. If you do these things, you will endure hardship and become a stronger, better person, and provide inspiration for others on their journey through adversity.

Chapter 12

# Free to Be Happy

I believe that happiness is what God wants for us most in this life. Simply, it is a divine right to find joy. Why then are so many people unhappy? We are often told by well-meaning people that happiness is a choice. So we are essentially expected to ignore all the adversity that is going on around us and *choose* to be happy. I am here to tell you that ignoring adversity is not a strategy to be happy. Forcing yourself to be happy does not work. It can work for a short time as you constantly control your thoughts, replacing the painful negative thoughts with positive ones. Unfortunately, the pain of adversity eventually creeps in and unhappiness follows. Now, don't misunderstand me. It is important, in fact critical, to choose not to entertain negative thoughts and allow them to become your focus. However, that is only one component to being happy and is not the entire solution to find joy in your life. Happiness is not a choice; it is a series of choices. Choosing to be positive and not dwell on the negative is one of those choices.

The secret to happiness is implementing certain things in your life in such a way that adversity simply has little impact. This book identifies many of those things: love, service, passion, etc. Additionally, lasting joy requires you to be in harmony spiritually with God in every way possible. I am not talking about obeying the Ten Commandments, which are important to many of us. It is not about being or acting a certain way. I am talking about understanding that you, as you are at this very moment, are perfect because God is perfect, and you are part of God. When you understand this, you then will be living life and finding joy *inside* of you and the things *outside* of you will have little impact. You will have diminished the impact of external things on your life. It is understanding that God's goal for you is happiness, and therefore, he is working with you to bring you happiness.

You must allow yourself to be happy. It is there waiting for you. You are the obstructionist of your own happiness. You, then, must *free* yourself to be happy.

What is freedom? Most of us would define freedom as being able to do and say whatever you want as long as it doesn't injure another person. Certainly this is an acceptable definition in most applications. I would like to redefine freedom somewhat. Freedom is the total absence of concern for oneself. I might add that the best way to have no concern for oneself is to have total concern for others.

Can you imagine living just one day without concern for yourself? No one bothering you with differing opinions, nothing angering you, no thought of achievement or acquiring of material things. No regret for the goals you did not achieve, no worry about what the future holds. You must admit that it sounds wonderful. That is freedom.

Is it even possible to live without thinking about yourself? I don't know, but it is a worthy goal. When you are not thinking about yourself, you can contribute so much more to the lives of others. Not just those most important to you, including your family and friends, but all those who can be affected by your life. That will bring you a pure joy that is impossible with the presence of ego or concern for oneself.

The first step is to eliminate your connection to your past. We all have done many things in the past that we regret. Things we wish we would or would not have done, people we wish we would have treated differently. Sometimes this can bring us pain. Perhaps even more damaging is that we think because we were a certain way in our past, we must be that way in our future. You must understand that your past brought you to this moment, and for that you must be grateful because from this moment on, life represents joy and happiness. From this point on, you are equipped to accept challenges and adversity for what they are, opportunities to strengthen you. Not painful occurrences that destroy your life.

When you get in a car, you have one thing in mind, your destination. You don't contemplate how the car was made. You don't worry about the mistakes in the past that were made building the car, the parts that may have been late getting to the factory delaying its production. You don't contemplate the flaws in the car that may be hidden. None of that matters. What matters is that it will take you to where you want to go.

The same is true for you. You need not worry about the mistakes that were made getting you to this point, only that you are fully equipped to get you where you need to go.

Let go of the past and embrace it with gratitude. It helped mold you for this moment.

Now let's talk about the future. Just as you are not your past, you are not your future. I believe that it is important to visualize where you want to go and who you want to be in the future. People often accept unhappiness today on the misguided notion that tomorrow will be better. But truly you can only control this very moment. The only thing you can do to impact your life is put your energy into this very moment. You have nothing else.

Let's continue on with the car metaphor. You really only have one thing in mind when you get in your car, right? Your destination. When you turn the key, you are not contemplating the many things that are going on in the background. Are the pistons firing appropriately? Is the oil reducing the friction at an acceptable level? No, you accept all that is happening in the background as a given and are only concerned with the destination. As you travel down the road, you never realize the many things that the car does to maintain your safety and ensure that you arrive at your destination. There are bumps you never feel. I would even bet that the far majority of bumps we never even notice, because the car absorbs them.

The same thing is true in our life. We have an idea of where we want to go but have no idea of the many things that are going on around us to ensure that we arrive at that destination. We are just blissfully driving along. You see, in life God has this vehicle with its infinite parts running smoothly. You must trust in him that the vehicle will get you where he wants you to go. Your Divine Source, God has everything under control. Just relax and enjoy the ride.

Look around you, look at the grass, the trees, the sky, the sun. All move in certain ways. A blade of grass will grow to be a blade of grass; the sun will rise on time, provide warmth, and set each day on schedule. The universe is organized, and just as the grass will be grass, the sun will be the sun, you will be you. Allow it to be so; trust that it will be so.

Let me challenge a conventional wisdom. In my world, the world where words and speech are meant to inspire and motivate, much is spoken about goals. Time management and goal setting are often subset topics taught by motivational speakers and self-help trainers. I believe it is important to set goals and develop a plan in which to reach those goals. But I also believe God always has a better way to get there and, in fact, may have a better goal for me that I may not even be aware of. External goals can actually be a deterrent to what is best for you. Be willing to accept direction from your Divine Source, which may alter your goals. This may come in the form of coincidences, intuition, inspired teachers, new visions put in your mind, or many other heavenly messengers. Allow your feelings to be the barometer of what is right for you. That still small voice that is inside each of us will confirm the correct path for you. When you are misaligned with God, you will feel uncomfortable, often without knowing why. If you continue down that path, being uncomfortable will progress to unhappiness and even depression. Alternatively, when you are aligned with God, you will feel comfort, which will lead to joy and happiness. Unfortunately, many of us spend time plowing through on our way to reaching our goals, only to be truly obstructing God's plan. When we reach our goal, we find we are unfulfilled. Think about it, how do you expect to know what is best for you when your view is so limited? Remember, "in the car of life" you only know how to get in the car, turn the key, and steer. There is so much more going on in the background that only your Divine Source understands; trust that he will get you there.

Instead make a commitment to enjoy this day a little more. Relax about the future and let it go. The more peaceful and calm you are, the more efficient and effective you will be, the more sensitive to the divine you will become, and the happier you will be.

# Free to be Happy

# Chapter 13

## Bounce Back

It was the fall of 2012 when we sat down to talk. Anna sat comfortably in the large puffy couch, wearing sweats and a blue tank top. Her lovely, dark brunette hair was tightly tied up in a ponytail, her legs crossed at the ankles, and she was holding a glass of wine in her right hand. At first cursory look when you see Anna, you are taken by her stunning good looks, but a closer look across her shoulders and down her arms reveals the scars of tragedy. The checkerboard scars don't diminish her beauty; in fact, as you get to know her they only enhance it. But it is clear there is a story behind those scars. A story of remarkable tragedy followed by inspirational courage.

Anna loved Noah. In 1997 she was twenty-four years old; he was a year younger at only twenty-three. Joy had finally come into both of their lives, and they saw a future filled with hope and love. Something neither of them had known much of in their past. Noah was an aikido master, having won many tournaments, a great accomplishment for such a young man. Anna was starting to enjoy success as a model.

Life was good.

Noah always drove the speed limit on his motorcycle, something not too many twenty-three-year-olds do. He also insisted Anna wear his black leather jacket when she rode with him. They were in a hurry because they needed to meet Anna's modeling representative in Barstow, California, to discuss an upcoming shoot. Anna had inadvertently left the jacket in her locker at work and they simply didn't have time to go get it. Noah insisted they go retrieve the jacket, but after some coaxing and stubbornness from Anna, she convinced him it was more important they be on time to the meeting.

It is amazing that such a simple decision can have a tremendous, lasting impact on one's life.

In just shorts and a tank top, Anna jumped on the back of the motorcycle, and they were off. At the same time a man driving a produce truck was running very late. He was driving recklessly and trying to make up time. As he came to a stop sign to cross Barstow Boulevard, he gave a brief tap of the brakes and then blew through the stop sign. That is when their two worlds met. Noah knew he was about to hit the side of the truck. Reaching back behind him just before they hit, he pushed Anna down to avoid the direct impact with the truck, probably saving her life. Noah wasn't so lucky and impacted the truck squarely; he was killed instantly. The truck sheered off the top of the motorcycle's gas can throwing all of its contents on Anna, and she ignited. She flew through the sky like a roman candle, flying through a tree, which caught on fire, and then landing in a field, some 125 feet away. It too caught on fire with Anna as its kindling. Perhaps most frightening of all was that Anna never lost consciousness.

At that moment she jumped up to go to Noah but couldn't walk because her knee was shattered. She tried again and again to get to him but kept falling, so she crawled. When she finally reached him, there was only that distant stare of a body without its spirit.

The paramedics arrived quickly and Life Flight not too long after. Anna's injuries were life threatening, and she needed serious medical help if she were to live. She was flown to San Bernardino Medical Center, which had a good burn ward. It was obvious she would need it. During the flight she started to slip in and out of consciousness.

In addition to serious head trauma and severe third-degree burns over her arms, chest, and head; she had a broken back, knee, ankle, scapula, ribs, and eye socket, with a partially dislocated eye, severed tongue, and shattered shoulder.

Anna was put into an induced coma over the next month. It was felt that the stress of the pain would simply be too much to endure and her body would give out. Anna's family had been told that the daughter, sister, and friend they knew was gone. She would never be able to hold a job performing anything but the most basic of requirements. There was just too much brain damage. Additionally, with the severity of the burns, the use of her arms would be extremely limited.

When Anna awakened, the challenge of a lifetime awaited her. The severe brain injury and coma left her with an erased memory. Imagine awaking from a sleep and not knowing anyone or anything. She had a faint memory of her two-year-old daughter but couldn't remember her name, and recalled that football season was just starting. That was it. She couldn't read; she couldn't speak. Her father, who hadn't left her side, was nameless. Her mother, sister, and best friend were all lost in her mind. And Noah? For the time being, there was no Noah.

As you will come to see, Anna is a very driven person. She started physical therapy, working on every part of her broken body. The pain was excruciating at every moment. She began to learn to read again, literally starting with "See Spot run. Run Spot run." Gentle movements of her arms were performed to try and rebuild her range of motion.

As time passed some of her memories were returning. The love for her two-year-old daughter began driving her, and Anna felt the pace of the therapy was too slow and began working on her own. She simply felt that unless she pushed harder she would never get out of the hospital. Her daughter needed her mother, and time was of the essence. The catheter was removed, and a bedside commode was the next step. She decided to skip that step and walk to the bathroom. With back brace, knee splint, and arms outstretched in burn dressings, she rose from her bed and pushed to the restroom. She must have been quite a sight. Exhausted when she entered the bathroom, she was startled because she thought there was someone else in there. She quickly realized that it was her own reflection in the mirror. She had not looked in a mirror since the accident. The one time model was now burned and covered in bandages to the point where she didn't recognize herself. She passed out, and the nurse found her lying on the bathroom floor.

After only six weeks in the hospital, Anna decided it was time to go home. It was sooner than the doctors wanted her to leave, but ultimately it was her decision. She felt that she would heal quicker by being with her daughter and having the support of her family. She had started remembering Noah and her love for him but hadn't been able to give it much thought. In fact, many memories had been coming back slowly. The doctor now felt that they could hasten that process with medication. For Anna, this was one of the most horrifying moments yet. Shortly after the medication was given, she started having a flood of memories coming at her from all parts of her life. There was no order or progression of thoughts. Some of the memories were terrifying and came at random and without explanation.

It was at that moment when she really

remembered Noah.

"Where is Noah?" she asked her father as she was going home. Scared of adding pain to his daughter's already painful life, he deflected the question. He wanted to tell her at home and in the company of her best friend, Dante. Anna deep down knew the answer to that question but was unable to think about it. When she arrived home, she asked her father again, this time in a firm, committed voice. "Where is Noah?"

Upon her father's answer, Anna no longer had just her physical pain to endure but the tremendous emotional pain from the death of the person she adored.

As she tells me this story some fifteen years later, her eyes fill with tears and her voice shudders. That didn't happen during the graphic description of the pain she endured from the burns and broken bones. It happened when she thought of Noah. I suspect Anna's greatest pain was the loss of Noah, a wound that never totally heals.

The next several months would be filled with unbelievable pain and anguish. The broken bones and torn tendons and muscles all began to heal. It was the brain injury and burns that would take the time and be the greatest challenge. Amazingly, Anna was able to get her first job as a home health aid only four months after the accident. After about a year she decided she needed even more independence, so she moved from Victorville to San Diego. She was on her own and building a new life. She loved to volunteer at the local burn center, giving hope to those just starting their painful journey.

As I spoke to Anna about the years of recovery, I was amazed at the repeated references to how grateful she was to so many people, and also to God. She remembered one of the first thoughts she had after the accident was one of gratitude to those who had saved her life. It became clear to me that Anna chose to be grateful rather than bitter and angry. That gratitude was certainly one of the great healers in her journey. Think about it, there was much to be angry about. She had lost her career, the love of her life, her physical and mental capacity. But she chose to find things for which to be grateful.

Anna decided she wanted to go back to school and become a massage therapist. Apparently she hadn't listened to the doctors when they told her she would only be able to do menial tasks because her brain would not function. Further, being a massage therapist would require tremendous strength, especially in her arms. Something that was supposedly impossible. Every weekday Anna would drop her daughter off at day care early, go to school for half the day, go to work until 6:00 p.m., pick up her daughter, care for her for a couple hours while trying to study some, put Brianna to bed, and believe it or not, go back to work for a few more hours. On Friday evening she would drive three hours to her father's home, leave her daughter there, and drive back to San Diego and work long hours all weekend. Sunday night she would make the same six-hour round trip again. This from a woman who just a couple years earlier was fighting for her life and still was healing from her injuries.

It was exhausting, and Anna was running out of energy and money. It was time for her final exam. This exam involved a detailed description and function of the human anatomy. It would challenge the most advanced of medical students, not to mention someone who had to relearn to read "Run Spot run" just a year or two earlier. She was down to her last seventeen dollars and had to pass the test so she could get a higher-paying job in massage therapy. If she didn't pass, she would not be able to continue because the test cost $250 to take and she had no resources left to pay for it. She had no other choice but to pass the test. Anna was scared to death as she opened the exam. She did her best to try and recall the many things she had studied so hard to learn, and after a couple hours completed the written exam. When it was time to get the results, she could only envision having failed and having to move back to inland California with her father, emphasizing the things she had been told. "You will never be able to hold a job...your brain is too damaged to achieve much in this life...you will never really be independent."

She failed the test.

All she had been told was true, she thought. As she walked out of the room with tears streaming down her face, obviously very upset, her instructor, James, stopped her. "Be here tomorrow at nine o'clock," he said. She tried to inquire as to why, but he simply restated, "Be here tomorrow at nine o'clock." Tomorrow was a Sunday and the school was closed on Sundays. Anna wasn't sure what to expect but trusted her teacher. She showed up on time, and James had unlocked the door to the school and to his classroom. As she walked in, he asked her to sit down and he placed the test in front of her. Anna started to explain that she just took the test yesterday and failed. James stopped her in mid-sentence and said with a wink-wink inflection, "You didn't take this test yesterday." He told her that he knew she understood the material and asked her to take a few minutes and get her head clear to take the test. Then he said, "Now take the test," suggesting that she could take the test and pass it this time. Still she opened the test with the anxiety of failure from the day before. James talked gently with her on the first couple answers, not helping her with the answers, but helping her to have confidence in her mind and herself.

She scored a 98 percent on the test.

To this day the kindness of her instructor, James, remains a pivotal moment in her life. She now knew that her brain injury could not hold her back from success. It was true that she may have to work harder than most people. But she knew that she could achieve great things, despite her injuries and despite the things she had been told by people who should "know" better. She was grateful for James teaching her that, perhaps the greatest lesson he could have taught her.

Anna next spoke to me about her spiritual journey through her challenges. She had been raised in a mildly religious home and always felt a connection to God, but hadn't developed her relationship with him.

When I first met Anna several years ago, I knew I had met a highly spiritual person. I could just feel it. I had no idea what her story was; I just felt this unconditional love emanate from her. It was only after having known her for a few years that I could understand why she was this way. In our discussions about her accident, she repeatedly referenced her gratitude to God for his help and for providing wonderful people like James to help her. I asked her if she ever felt angry at God for putting her through this challenge. She acted almost confused at the question. You see, for Anna, God only represents the path by which she overcame her tribulations. He saved her from her tragedy. You see, Anna understands that she and God are inseparable; they are one, and together they can achieve anything. She also believes that she is one and part of all people, who are also one with God. This gives her a tremendous love for people. That is what I felt those years ago when I first met her.

By developing her relationship with God and making spirituality a part of her life, she found a positivity that surrounded her regardless of her challenges. She was able to take that positivity and become more than just the person who nearly died from a tragic motorcycle accident. Her accident would not define her; it would only be something she went through. Many people become defined by their tragedy. By that I mean it becomes something that is attached to who they are. Strangely, when that happens, people can be stalled in their healing. By labeling who they are by what they have gone through, it can make them relive the process, or even nurture their own ego for having endured the tragedy. I found this to be true after my wife died. I became the poor widower with three very young children. You begin to play the part and stay in that role. It feels good because you get sympathy and accolades for being a "survivor." But in reality you remain a victim of what happened to you. When you are a victim, you lose control of your life. To attain true happiness you must be responsible and control your life.

Anna continued to grow spiritually and intellectually as the years passed by. Physically, she is quite remarkable. She had always been very strong physically and had confidence that she would again be so. Throughout her rehab she worked intensely on building her strength. Last time I checked, the primary requirement for being a massage therapist is having extraordinary strength in one's arms. Is there a less likely field in which Anna would be successful? Maybe being a female kick boxer. Oh wait, did I mention that Anna is also a kick boxer and personal trainer? Yes, in addition to being a successful massage therapist, she is a certified personal trainer with amazing strength and agility...and a kick boxer.

This is not to say that Anna's struggles are not

ongoing. At times she has memory loss and moments of complete confusion. But she presses on in those moments and radiates a spirit of positivity that I have rarely seen. It took years of intense dedication and both physical and emotional endurance, but Anna today is a remarkable woman who has risen above life's greatest challenges.

But what about Noah, the love of her life? She never felt that she would meet someone like Noah and accepted that as a part of her life. She met good men who wanted to spend their lives with her. She hoped she could feel a love for them, enough love to have a good, lifetime relationship. But they would never be Noah. It just never quite worked out. Until Dan.

She had known Dan for a few years. Both of them were in different places in life and they never considered each other romantically. Dan was someone she enjoyed talking to mostly as a client; she was a lovely woman from whom Dan received massage therapy. But then it changed. Dan spontaneously asked her out, they dated and quickly fell madly in love and married.

Recently I attended Anna's fortieth birthday party. It was a remarkable event. Dan had rented the ballroom at a hotel, hired a live band, and invited friends who flew in from all over the country to be there, because they love Anna and Dan.

After a few hours of dancing, Dan stood in front of the crowd to offer a toast to his sweetheart. He talked about how he had waited so many years, had gone through so many experiences, hoping to find her. He had been in love before but still never felt what he felt at that moment, absolute true love for Anna. He adored her.

The beautiful thing is that as I am sitting with Anna and she is sitting on that big fluffy couch in her sweats, legs crossed, holding a glass of wine, her eyes sparkling as she talks about meeting the love of her life...again, Dan.

Life is filled with challenges and adversity. Most of us will never have to endure and overcome what Anna did. This is not to minimize our own challenges. All of us at some point will deal with difficulties that may seem overwhelming.

Shortly after the death of my wife, a person said, "At least you didn't get divorced." He had the strange belief that my healthy, loving marriage that was torn apart by death was not as bad as going through a divorce. I remember being completely stunned by that comment.

While I still think that comment was not the best thing to say, it is clear that it was a difficult moment, and it was his attempt at consoling me. Additionally, I have a very different viewpoint now than I did all those years ago when my first wife died. I have since gone through a devastating divorce. The pain truly was extraordinary. I loved my wife very much but knew that it was the right thing to divorce her. The pain was very different from the death of my first wife, but it really was just as intense. In my wildest dreams, I never thought a divorce could be as painful as the death of a spouse. In my case, it was.

After the divorce I was laying on my bed and tears were streaming down my face. I was really hurting. After some time in this emotional state, I sat up to try and catch my breath and regain my composure. As I sat on the edge of my bed, I almost subconsciously reached over and grabbed a red ball that was sitting on my nightstand. My thoughts were elsewhere, but I just started bouncing the ball against my wall and catching it. I bounced it and caught it again. I did this several times. Then I stopped and looked at the ball. I slowly reached over and opened my nightstand drawer and pulled out a black Sharpie marker. Pulling the cap off the top, I carefully wrote on the ball, "I BOUNCE BACK."

"*I bounce back.*" That was it, that is what I would do. That was a pivotal moment of my life. It was at that time I decided that my life would change and I would find joy. It was at that moment I started my journey to discover how I could be happy during the difficult times of adversity with which life challenged me. While it has taken a few years of growing and tremendous effort, I can truly say I am unbelievably happy, even though, at this time, my life is filled with adversity.

Trust me, you may be in financial ruin, struggling from the death of a loved one, be sick or alone, in a job you hate, or simply, just painfully sad; but you can still rise above it and find joy. Find something you are passionate about and participate in it every day; find love for yourself and others. Look for opportunities to provide service. Don't let fear dictate your actions. Allow yourself to be free of your past, and you will feel joy.

I know this isn't easy and you may require the help of others. There are times when you may not feel so strong. There will be times that negativity and sadness will creep into your life. Remember your goals, engage your Bounce Back strategies, and move forward.

By the way, the red ball still sits on my nightstand and reminds me every day that I Bounce Back.

# About the Author

Jack W. Ryser is the father of three beautiful daughters and considers them to be his greatest success. After many successful, and some not-so-successful, years in business, Jack trained to be a Life Coach and started his company, Jack Ryser Personal Development. His Life Coaching practice primarily focuses on working with those who have suffered a significant loss, often death or divorce, and helping them move on to have a wonderful life.

Jack is an inspirational public speaker and often is featured at corporate retreats, charitable events, and conferences. He also can be found teaching seminars and workshops, both live and online. He is always eager to correspond with his readers. Feel free to contact him at jack@jackryser.com or visit his website at jackryser.com.